'We've all met 1 [...] [pro-]
vocative essay, S[...] who
publicly spout feminism while treating women badly
behind closed doors — and asks how we can move
forward to a happier, more feminist future.'

SAMANTHA ELLIS

'Sam Mills has given us an update on the #MeToo
movement. Thought-provoking, on point and abreast
of contemporary ideas about the chauvinism of women's
everyday lives. A book for our times.'

MONIQUE ROFFEY

'A *cri de coeur* written from the precipice of a new
cultural landscape... In this lithe and luminous essay,
Sam Mills explodes the hypocrisy of many men in the
wake of the #MeToo movement. Here she deftly blends
her own experiences at the hands of one such "chauvo-feminist" with a critique of what really constitutes
social change regarding the abuse of women by powerful
men. Clever, funny, gripping and beautifully written,
*Chauvo-Feminism* is an exploration not just of the female
experience, but of civilisation itself. This is a dazzling,
essential book. Men with mutant politics: beware!'

EMMA JANE UNSWORTH

# CHAUVO-
# FEMINISM

# CHAUVO-FEMINISM

*On Sex, Power
and #MeToo*

SAM MILLS

THE
INDIGO
PRESS

THE INDIGO PRESS

50 Albemarle Street
London W1S 4BD
www.theindigopress.com

The Indigo Press Publishing Limited Reg. No. 10995574
Registered Office: Wellesley House, Duke of Wellington Avenue
Royal Arsenal, London SE18 6SS

COPYRIGHT © SAM MILLS 2021

This edition first published in Great Britain in 2021 by The Indigo Press

Sam Mills asserts the moral right to be identified as the author of this
work in accordance with the Copyright, Designs and Patents Act 1988

A CIP catalogue record for this book is available from the British Library

ISBN: 978-1-911648-18-5
eBook ISBN: 978-1-911648-21-5

All rights reserved. No part of this publication may be reproduced,
stored in a retrieval system or transmitted, in any form or by any means,
electronic, mechanical, photocopying, recording or otherwise, without
the prior permission of the publishers.

Design by houseofthought.io
Typeset in Goudy Old Style by Tetragon, London
Printed and bound in Great Britain by TJ Books Limited, Padstow

MIX
Paper from
responsible sources
FSC® C013056

*For L.K.*

The experiences described in this essay, whether mine or the women I interviewed, are all true. However, dates, names, places and other details may have been changed to protect the privacy, and conceal the identities, of certain individuals.

Women's liberation has often been portrayed as a movement intent on encroaching upon or taking power and privilege away from men, as though in some dismal zero-sum game, only one gender at a time could be free and powerful. But we are free together or slaves together.

—REBECCA SOLNIT,
'The Longest War' (2013)

# I

Late spring, the late 1990s: I am sitting in a small conference room in Oxford University. I am nineteen years old. There are eleven students in our group, twice as many men as women. We are in our first year studying for a BA in English Literature.

The tutor enters. She is in her mid-fifties, tall and elegant, with salt-and-pepper hair and shrewd eyes. She sits down and informs us that she is standing in for this lesson because our usual tutor is absent. We are here to discuss feminist literary theory.

We all take a look at the photocopied extracts we have been given in preparation: an essay by Susan Gubar called '"The Blank Page" and the Issues of Female Creativity'. She asks if we have any opinions on this. A silence follows. I feel uncomfortable; hesitant. I am one of the few people at my college from a working-class background. I still feel as though I am lucky to be at Oxford rather than someone who belongs there. Though

I am confident when I pick up a pen and shape an essay, I am unpractised at translating my opinions into articulate speech. Many of the male students in my group have grown up being taught to debate at private school. Some look as though they wouldn't be out of place in a Bullingdon Club photo. Usually they dominate the discussions, locking intellectual antlers. The silence feels conspiratorial: a pact of rejection.

And then one of the men mutters, 'I think she's got a clitoris problem,' and a snigger ripples through the group. He gives the tutor a sidelong glance to emphasize that it is *her* particular clitoris that offends him.

I'm not sure if the tutor has heard him. She chooses to ignore him. She carries on with the lesson, but it is not a success. Every so often, a female student engages with her, but the men remain unusually quiet.

I feel bewildered by what I have witnessed. I have spent my teenage years studying at a girls' school. I have grown up with brothers, in a household full of men who have treated me with respect. My experience of the male sex has been compartmentalized: I have danced with boys, dated them, got drunk with them, but I have not had to sit in a room with them and compete, nor deal with waspish remarks about female genitalia. My mother was discouraged from studying for a degree because her chauvinistic father said it was a waste of time and money, declaring she would only end up getting married and having kids. She has made it clear that I am different:

I am from a privileged generation. I am under the illusion that I have prepared myself for my degree because I have spent my holidays industriously devouring the greats of English literature, from *Beowulf* to Chaucer to Austen to Eliot. I have not studied de Beauvoir, or Greer, or Wolf due to the idealistic assumption that times have evolved: we are living in a world that has undergone several waves of feminism and is now egalitarian.

Sitting in that room in Oxford, I felt as though I had been launched into a battlefield without armour, weaponry or training, to fight a war that I thought women of decades past had already won.

Whenever I retell this experience, people immediately assume that the chauvinist I am describing is a supercilious public school boy. But he had studied at a comprehensive, seemed down to earth, had a good sense of humour and was well liked.

In our next tutorial, he argued passionately against having to study feminist literary theory at all. The tutor pointed out that such a line of argument would mean there was also no point in studying post-colonialism, or having any interest in anyone beyond his own small sphere of experience. This did not seem to strike him as a problem.

If I were to see my chauvinist again – at a reunion, for example – I am sure that he would be deeply embarrassed about his remarks, just as I feel angry with my young self for staying silent. He is happily married now, a successful professional, and behaves in a respectful manner with his female colleagues. We were all intelligent students, but we were also naïve teenagers. By the time I left Oxford, I was what I might describe as a feminist-in-the-making, still under-read and confused by a world that was not as egalitarian as I thought it, but ready to fight if need be.

The 1990s to early 2000s was an era where female rights moved forward and backward. Rebecca Walker sparked feminism's 'third wave' when she responded to Anita Hill giving testimony against Judge Clarence Thomas, who had received a Supreme Court nomination. Hill accused him of sexual harassment when they had worked together in the years 1981–3. Though Thomas was still confirmed as an associate justice, there was a public wave of anger at the way Hill was demeaned and dismissed by an all-male, all-white Senate Judiciary Committee. Walker published a piece in Ms Magazine entitled 'Becoming the Third Wave', in which she argued that Hill's treatment was not about Thomas's guilt, but 'checking and defining the extent of women's credibility and power'. She declared: 'I am not a postfeminism feminist. I am the Third Wave.' This wave celebrated Girl Power and the importance of intersectionality, coined by Kimberlé Williams Crenshaw. Eve Ensler's The Vagina Monologues were first performed on stage; Thelma and Louise hit cinemas and became an instant feminist classic; Susan Faludi published the iconic *Backlash*. In the US, huge strides forward were made in politics. Janet Reno became the first female Attorney General; Madeleine Albright the first Secretary of State. And in business Carly Fiorina became the CEO of Hewlett-Packard, the first female CEO of a Fortune 100 company.

But the 1990s was also a decade of lads' mags, where topless women in skimpy thongs grinned out from the magazine shelves in supermarkets. It was a decade when virtually anything a female author penned ended up with a pink cover and being pitched as the next *Bridget Jones*, regardless of whether it was trash or quality literature, as though women writers and readers were a flock of sheep whose only interests were happy endings and Manolo heels. It was the era when *Men Are from Mars, Women Are from Venus* sold in millions, asserting every gender stereotype going, followed by increasingly absurd copycat titles which declared that women couldn't read maps or men were unable to cry, all backed up by 'scientific research'. And it was an era in which – as Natasha Walter explores in *Living Dolls* – feminist movements were appropriated to sell and market male fantasies. Hence, it became 'empowering' for a woman in a struggling financial predicament to dance naked around a pole to a room of men in suits with plenty of money in their pockets; it became 'empowering' for women to enter the *Nuts* magazine 'Babes on the Bed' competition and writhe around on a bed in front of a cheering male crowd, stripping off in the hope of a modelling contract.

All this laid the foundations for the fourth wave of feminism that began circa 2012. Like my experience in the Oxford tutorial, women were waking up and noting the vast gap between ideals and reality. 'It's no surprise that a generation of women who were brought up being told that they were equal to men, that sexism, and therefore feminism was dead [were] starting to see through this,' Kira Cochrane observed.

Fast-forward twenty years from my uni days, and how far we seem to have come. If I were sitting in a conference room in an Oxford college today, and a male student made a remark about a female tutor having a *clitoris problem*, I suspect that there would be an outcry from fellow students, a Twitter shitstorm and disciplinary action for the perpetrator.

Lads' mags have been taken off the shelves. Feminist movements have sprung up all over the world, from Laura Bates' Everyday Sexism Project to Caroline Criado-Perez's fight for a female face on a banknote to Pussy Riot hunger-striking in Russia to protests in India after a gang rape on a bus to a pushback against unfair pay. Novelists such as Zoe Pilger and Nicole Flattery are writing about young women negotiating sex and relationships without their work being pigeonholed as 'chick lit', as I believe it would have been two decades ago. Sally Rooney and Sophie Mackintosh were featured on the Booker Prize longlist, while Bernardine Evaristo was the first black woman to win the prize with *Girl, Woman, Other*. No More Page 3 demonstrations have sprung up around the country. The Presidents Club hit the headlines when their all-male 'charity fundraiser' involved attractive young women having to serve powerful, wealthy men who groped and assaulted them with the casualness of entitlement, as if reaching for a tray of canapés. The dinner, which has run for decades, died a death overnight in the ensuing scandal. The #MeToo movement, initially created by Tarana Burke, was a revolutionary moment: a tidal wave of confessions, a cleansing of repressions ignored for decades. It highlighted how important the internet has been in this fourth wave of feminism, albeit a space ferociously fought over by feminists and those opposing them.

In the revelations that followed the #MeToo campaign, I was struck by how often men who abused women lived double lives. Their surface persona was frequently that of the nice guy anchored by marriage, the feminist male who championed equality, while their shadowy doppelgänger would often be hitting women or assaulting them or belittling them or undermining them.

Human beings are complex creatures and we inevitably suffer a tragic gap between our ideals and our behaviour; but when that gap becomes too yawningly wide, we name it hypocrisy.

Take Eric Schneiderman. What an inspiration he seemed, before his fall. He was the sixty-fifth New York Attorney General. A champion of women's rights. He filed a civil rights suit against Harvey Weinstein and was a key figure in bringing him to justice, fighting for his victims to get greater compensation. He appeared at events supporting reproductive freedom. He wrote a bill which specifically punished the crime of strangulation after he chaired a committee that investigated domestic violence. When journalists Ronan Farrow, Jodi Kantor and Megan Twohey shared a joint Pulitzer Prize for their groundbreaking reporting on Weinstein, Schneiderman tweeted his support and congratulations, praising 'the brave women and men who spoke up about the sexual harassment they had endured at the hands of powerful men'.

In May 2018, the *New Yorker* ran an exposé that showed another side to Schneiderman. Four women described how they had been slapped and choked, mocked and abused by him. Michelle Manning Barish, one of his exes, remarked, 'You cannot be a champion of women when you are hitting them and choking them in bed, and saying to them, "You're a fucking whore".' Schneiderman's initial response was that he had just been 'role-playing', asserting 'I have not assaulted anyone. I have never engaged in non-consensual sex, which is a line I would not cross.' Within three hours of the allegations, he had resigned.

Take Harvey Weinstein. He once went on a women's march at Sundance, marching in the same vicinity as the hotel where he'd allegedly raped Rose McGowan years earlier. He helped to endow a faculty chair at Rutgers University in the name of feminist icon Gloria Steinem. In 2015, the Weinstein Company distributed a film called *The Hunting Ground*, a documentary about campus sexual assault, the same year that Lauren O'Connor wrote her memo condemning the toxic culture towards women at his workplace. There is a striking moment in the documentary *Untouchable: The Rise and Fall of Harvey Weinstein* where Weinstein turns up at a luncheon fundraiser for Hillary Clinton. The documentary shows a picture of him seated between two women, grinning away, this man who had raped a woman and made demands such as 'show me your breasts' with the warning '*Do you know who I am? I can make your career or I can break your career.*' The female journalist being interviewed, Rebecca Traister – who was once the victim of an irrational fit of Weinstein's rage when he called her a cunt for no good reason – recounted that at this point in his career, Harvey's power was waning. Seeing him, she mused: 'You're putting your money towards protecting yourself, positioning yourself as a feminist, as an ally to powerful women.' She concluded in angry resignation: 'Nobody was ever going to win against this guy.' After the allegations against Weinstein were made public, he issued a statement asserting, 'I so respect women', and declared that all the encounters with his accusers were consensual. He also made a point of highlighting that he was setting up a foundation to give scholarships to women directors at the University of Southern California, assuring us that: 'While this might seem coincidental, it has been in the works for a year…'

Even Aziz Ansari – billed as the nice guy with a Netflix show who emphasized the importance of treating women well – ended up being publicly shamed on babe. net after a disastrous date with a girl (who went by the pseudonym Grace) ended in foreplay that he enjoyed and she regarded as assault. The story is an ambiguous one, fraught with misunderstandings, highlighting how complex the nuances of consent can be, and has prompted much debate as to whether Ansari really did deserve to be villainized. Aziz's response to the piece was that he had thought the evening was 'by all indications completely consensual' and was 'surprised and concerned. I took her words to heart and responded privately after taking the time to process what she had said.' However, he did not appear to express much sensitivity to Grace when he lifted her hand onto his dick five to seven times after she moved it away, and asked her for a blow job after she'd told him, 'I don't want to feel forced' and conveyed how uncomfortable she was. The trigger that caused Grace to 'out' him and share her story, when approached by babe.net? She saw Aziz wearing a Time's Up pin at the Golden Globe Awards in January 2018. She was furious that a man whose 'feminism' was on display in the form of a badge conducted a private life of pure contradiction.

There are, of course, many men who support feminism in theory and in practice. They tweet it and mean it. Their daily lives reflect their ideals. Such men should be applauded. In our wrath over Weinstein, we should not forget to celebrate male feminist heroes. Andy Murray, for example, has regularly challenged casual sexism in the sports world, arguing for equal pay for men and women in tennis, and correcting the sloppy and casual sexism of journalists. When congratulated on being the first person to win two Olympic gold medals in tennis, he pointed out, 'I think Venus and Serena have won about four each.' There are men who have reacted with such intelligence and maturity to the #MeToo movement, such as the actor Justin Baldoni, who has discussed the issue in a series of talks called Man Enough on his YouTube channel and inspired men to join him.

There are men, too, who are struggling to adjust to the rapid changes in society. They have spent decades enjoying the safety net of the patriarchy, and suddenly they have been forced to grow up painfully fast. Gender stereotypes are being overturned. Patriarchal power dynamics are crumbling. Some men can be motivated by a sincere intent to keep up, but they blunder and make mistakes without intentional malice as they develop emotional literacy. In this hysterical age where one poorly worded tweet can incite a mob, forgiveness is a virtue. We are all on a journey together, all learning, and I myself have discarded beliefs I held in my twenties that feel like an embarrassment now. As we react to a changing cultural climate, there has to be room for debate, for mistakes to be made and confusion dispersed.

But for those men who are private abusers and public champions of women's rights, feminism has become a convenient mask. To quote Mark Twain, 'history does not repeat but it does rhyme'. Just as female empowerment was commandeered in the 1990s by lad culture, now the #MeToo movement is being appropriated in our current era by certain abusers who conceal their chauvinism under the veil of a woke persona.

Recently I was having dinner with a female friend when she told me about a man she had gone for a drink with some years back. He had initially seemed pleasant, but when she'd got to his flat, he'd tried to coerce her into a bizarre and violent sexual act. She had asked to leave and called a cab. (Her story is described in more detail a little later in this essay.)

She recalled how she had spotted this same man tweeting during the Weinstein scandal. He'd asserted how disgraceful it was and how much sympathy he had for the wronged women.

She had thought about calling him out on this, but then decided against it: 'The trouble with outing a man is that it can define you. That's how you become known to the public.'

And I told my friend that I too had encountered a man just like him.

A chauvo-feminist.

Everyone I know says they've met a chauvo-feminist at some point during the past few years. I've met women who have been their victims, and men who have observed their bad behaviour.

A chauvo-feminist is the abusive man who hides in plain sight. Aware that his misogyny would not be tolerated in the current climate, conscious that it could end in the destruction of his reputation and career, he constructs a persona, a screen of smoke and mirrors. His misogyny is careful; it is compartmentalized. He will have female friends who are his allies and alibis, asserting what a great guy he is. His chauvinism is select, targeted at women whom he can manipulate easily, whom he perceives as lacking the power to stand up to him. His undermining of women is subtle. The day after he subjects a woman to emotional abuse, he will tweet or put a post on Facebook about how supportive he is of female empowerment and the destruction of the patriarchy.

Ultimately, this type of chauvinism represents a new problem for women in its deceit and its subtlety. When I consider the problems that I faced in my encounter with a chauvo-feminist, they were much harder to untangle and address compared to a man who simply spouted the silly line that the woman teaching him had a clitoris problem.

The chauvinism of the past might have been crude and overt, but it was easier to pinpoint and label. The chauvinism of the present, driven underground, is more insidious and harder to fight. Just when women have been given the empowerment of being able to speak out on social media, the chauvo-feminist can undermine it. Or, if 'outed', he has sufficient armour, in his persona and his string of feminist tweets, to create doubt about his behaviour – *could the guy who has attacked misogynist movements and tweeted so many links to female causes really be that bad?*

The chauvo-feminist is one of the new challenges that women face in the battle for equality.

The first half of my essay will explore abuse and gaslighting, and in the second half I will consider this in light of the impact and aftermath of the #MeToo movement.

My story is not a #MeToo confession. While I suffered emotional abuse at the hands of a chauvo-feminist, mine is not a tale of non-consensual sexual transgression. Yet I have felt the profound impact of the cultural change brought about by #MeToo on my life. It influenced my ability to intellectualize and process my difficult experiences with a chauvo-feminist. It gave me the courage eventually to fight back against him.

## II

This is a true account in which some names, details and locations have been changed. R is a pseudonym. His real name does not begin with this letter.

When I first met R, I wasn't particularly attracted to him. I was staying in Lancashire, on a break from the capital city, when a friend invited me along to a summer party in Manchester. When I arrived, I found I knew no one there. I was introduced to R: a British academic who was based at an American university. His accent sounded upper middle class. He seemed very charming, though we spoke for only a few minutes.

At the end of the evening, when the gathering had that blurry, tipsy atmosphere of a spiralling-down party, R found me in a small corridor, waiting for the toilet. There was a mirror on the wall and I was combing my messy hair. R wandered up and static swished strands into his face; I apologized; he twisted a strand of my hair around his finger and smiled. I laughed. I was charmed by him. The next day, we connected online.

Every day, we exchanged eight to ten emails. We discussed dreams, teenage lovers, childhood memories. I felt aroused but frustrated because I could no longer concentrate on my writing; my finger kept pressing the refresh key on my inbox.

I showed the emails to a friend, who observed, 'Well, this is clearly a guy who wants a relationship, not a one-night stand.'

I did not want a relationship. I was still raw from a romance of three and a half years that had recently ended. I felt inexperienced in the new complexities of internet dating; I told my friend that I'd forgotten how to flirt. My life was also fettered by responsibility: I was now a carer for my elderly father, who suffered from schizophrenia. And yet one-night stands were not my habit, either. I found myself picturing negotiations and wondering if he would accept some sort of liminal, vague exclusive-but-not-intense fuck-buddy friendship type of thing.

Pinning down our first date felt like a step backward and a step forward: would reality burst our online bubble? He had suggested I go to his flat; he was renting one for the summer before he returned to the USA for the fall semester.

As I walked past a row of Edwardian houses on a plush street, I realized how wealthy he must be. Inside, his pad was similar to mine, messy and librarial. As he poured us drinks, I wandered about, examining the piles of books. I picked out one that had been written by a friend of mine who was in academia. Let's call this academic Chloë, though that is not her real name. I was surprised when R told me that he knew her, having met her at a conference some months ago.

R and I shared kisses on his couch. Then caresses. We were slipping into a dream haze when he suddenly drew out his mobile phone. He showed me a picture of a blonde woman he had been seeing for the past few weeks. All her internet dating profile pics were of her in swimsuits, showing off an hourglass figure. She had wanted a relationship, R explained, but he hadn't been interested. I realized the subtext to his words: our encounter this evening would just be casual. I experienced both relief and disappointment that I would not need to worry about a man seeking commitment.

Yet there was a narcissistic pride in the way he was showcasing his ex to me, like the photographs you see of a man who enjoys shooting wildlife and stands next to the carcass of a beautiful slain lioness. Furthermore, R did not ask me what I wanted. Rather, he was determined to assert that what we were about to do was casual, whether I liked it or not. The narrative, he assumed, was his to dictate. I sensed both egotism and vulnerability, as though he was attempting to simultaneously seduce and reject me.

Then R suggested we go upstairs.

I've had plenty of time to analyse events since they occurred. Looking back, I feel like shouting at the 'me' of that evening and telling her to put down her glass, pull on her coat and go home. But in the present, things move fast. There was little time for reflection. I was guided more by desire than reason. We'd shared weeks of internet foreplay. To head home would seem like an anticlimax; therefore, I had to nudge aside the warning signs. A one-night stand was something I had rarely enjoyed and the adventurer inside me rallied me to be a liberated woman, enjoy the night, go with the flow.

We were in the middle of making love when he mentioned Chloë. He had slept with her, he confessed. He looked pleased with himself when he told me that. After he had climaxed, he elaborated their story with a little more detail. He'd been keen to just be friends with her, so it had been very awkward for him when she'd come on to him. He had yielded. Had sex with her. He didn't want it to happen again. But he did add the postscript: 'I don't think there are many men who can say they've slept with two writers who are good friends.' And then he smirked.

I concealed my hurt with nonchalance. I reminded myself that this was a casual fling, nothing more. I thought back to the party where I had first met R and the way I had idly watched him sidling from one woman to another. He had looked like a man on the prowl; he had also seemed a little sad and lonely to me. If he was promiscuous, then I wasn't going to judge him.

I sensed that he had carved out a part for me. If one-night stands were his fetish, then he had a script he wanted women to play. He was meant to be the rake and I his victim. He wanted to be smart and render me naïve. I decided to resist this role, yet my retaliation was a strange one. I found myself mirroring him. Rewriting my persona and acting as though I, too, was promiscuous and easy come, easy go. I told him that I did not believe in monogamy and fidelity when in truth my thoughts on the subject were a lot more uncertain – and veered far more towards the traditional – than I asserted. It was a way of refusing to allow him the victory of sadism; it was also a way of not running away from his bed. Despite everything, I was enjoying the physical pleasure of having sex with him.

And when he wasn't detailing all his conquests, he could be charming. Often, just when I wanted to slap him, he'd perform a U-turn. He'd cuddle me, compliment me, tease me sweetly. I wanted to see the night through, even if it was imperfect, even if the pleasure was laced with pain.

Sometime in the early hours, he surrendered his desire for caddish control and allowed himself a rare moment of vulnerability. He spoke about a difficult divorce that had occurred three, four years ago, from a woman whom he had clearly adored. He looked close to tears, and I hugged him. I reflected that he wasn't the first man I'd met who, rather than working through his pain, had reacted by sleeping with woman after woman as an attempt to suture a wound.

Morning came, and we had an amicable breakfast in a café near his flat. We spoke about writing. He looked both admiring and cross when I told him that I began every morning by writing several thousand words. It turned out that he wanted to enhance his career by becoming an author. He'd published several academic works, but he was keen to write a novel. He added that he knew a few people in publishing; R, it seemed, was one of those well-connected types who knew someone in every industry.

We said our goodbyes, exchanging kisses on the cheek.

I had no regrets about sleeping with him, for all his bad behaviour. 'It was a fun night,' I told various friends, keen to digest this narrative myself, to blot out the darker moments. I carried on exchanging flirty messages with him, pondered on the possibilities of a second one-night stand.

I believed that R and I could be friends, not realizing that the night had left him unsatisfied in some way. I had, after all, refused to play the role of a victim, a woman humiliated. And, as I was to learn, this created a frustration that continued to simmer inside him.

First came the rejection.

A fortnight later, I met him at a party. Chloë had invited him along. R was funny, charming and popular, telling amusing anecdotes and ingratiating himself into the group. With me, he was different. For much of the night, he played a game of contradiction. He flirted with me, yet told me how keen he was for me to date his friend. His friend, he informed me, had a better attitude to women than him, for he didn't 'sleep with women he didn't really like'. At the end of the evening, R took great pleasure in advising me that he would not be spending the night with me but was going on to another party. I looked at the gleam in his eyes and realized how important it was for him to reject me; I shrugged and nodded goodbye.

I had had enough.

I was becoming bored by his predictable unpredictability. I realized that adopting a carefree persona and feigning nonchalance towards his bad behaviour was an error of judgement. My self-esteem was still his punchbag, and I was on some level legitimizing his behaviour. Friendship, I concluded, was the simplest solution.

A few weeks on, I bumped into R at a bookshop reading in London. The author, publisher and audience ended up going on to a nearby pub afterwards.

All of a sudden, R approached and clumsily introduced me to someone who I'd call an important figure in the literary world. He was someone who ran residencies, who was looking for writers to be guest lecturers on his creative writing courses.

'I've been dying to matchmake you all night,' R said to us, italicizing the word 'matchmake' with pointed innuendo. I saw the glint of a wedding ring on the man's hand and suddenly panicked. He looked uneasy, too, as though R was a pimp who had brought him a courtesan he hadn't asked for. I blurted out a story about having a boyfriend; he blurted back that he had a wife. We both attempted thereafter to have a conversation about literary matters, but it was stilted and ridiculously polite.

Angry with R, I brought up his odd behaviour over email. His swift response was, 'It's all in your head.' Then we started to chat and flirt again via email, and soon we were back to our former pattern. R had succeeded in making me rewrite events so that they fit with his narrative. I thought to myself: *I was clearly mistaken. It was just cross-purposes. R made a perfectly innocent introduction, and I misunderstood.* I brushed away all doubts with the conviction that I had been paranoid, mistaken, oversensitive. I tried to ignore the fact that R had undermined my career, clouded an introduction to someone I would normally have been thrilled to meet.

Social media was another factor that helped me to invest in his narrative. He tweeted links to feminist articles. Retweeted pro-female pieces. I looked at them and persuaded myself that he was a little fucked up but basically a decent guy, one who had to like women if he supported feminist causes.

# III

One of my favourite novels when I was growing up was the classic *Les Liaisons Dangereuses* by Pierre Choderlos de Laclos. Two bored aristocrats, the Marquise de Merteuil and the Vicomte de Valmont, scheme to seduce and destroy the reputations of various men and women through amorous games. The Marquise de Merteuil is an extraordinary character: cruel, controlling, cynical, and acutely conscious of the limitations that society places on her gender. As a young girl, she found herself 'condemned by my status to silence and inaction'. She has learned to adopt masks, to perfect the subtle arts of manipulation, in order to survive in a society where one wrong word from the opposite sex could bring her down. Valmont is also a glittering character: a witty rake, louche, careless and dangerously attractive. He is enticed by Merteuil to deflower the virginal daughter of her enemy; the scene of seduction veers uneasily between rape and consent.

By the end of the book, everyone is fucked, literally and metaphorically. Valmont is both humanized and destroyed when he falls in love with one of his victims, the pious, innocent and religious Madame de Tourvel. His redemption leads to his death.

In comparison to Laclos' masterpiece, Francine Pascal's *Caitlin* trilogy is page-turning trash. But at the age of fifteen, I lapped it up. The eponymous heroine is beautiful and ruthless and bitchy. Having been brought up by her cruel, wealthy grandmother, she behaves incorrigibly. She steals the handsome, wholesome Jed from another girl at her boarding school and accidentally cripples a child. Caitlin writes a lengthy letter of confession to Jed, who finds it by accident. He decides that he will punish her by taking her virginity at the school prom. As they make out in the gazebo, he gropes her and tells her that he is going to 'take advantage of her'. Rape will be her punishment. The dubious philosophy behind this did not worry me too much; the scenario was presented as thrilling, and I was actually rather disappointed when Jed lost his nerve on the night, declaring that he could not go through with his plan.

This was my literary diet, growing up: glorious bad boys. Desirable rakes and innocent women. The joy of being preyed upon. Women pretending they didn't want sex when they did. Sex and violence entwined and presented as a seductive cocktail.

I am not condemning these books for their portrayal of men and women. Good novels present the complexity of life, not ideals; they mirror and comment on human nature; the above examples pinpoint certain moments in society. They illustrate how much things have changed. But, as a bookworm, I grew up seeking life advice in literature and took its lessons far too earnestly. One might have imagined that my romantic life was entirely doomed from this point on. Fortunately, I had sufficient self-respect to believe that I deserved to be treated well; I enjoyed being chased by men who loved me as well as lusted after me. But rakes always intrigued me, and I never forgot what an attractive aura art had painted around them.

R and I were still flirting with each other online. But I wanted to establish myself in a new compartment in R's mind, one in which I might move from 'prey' to 'equal' to 'liked'.

It was hard to know if I succeeded in this, for whenever I saw him that summer he swerved from being cool and critical to effusively warm and pleasant. On one occasion, he rubbished a book that I was publishing at the indie press I co-ran, even though he hadn't even read it; on another, he greeted me with warmth and hugs and teasing affection.

Chloë, our mutual friend, spoke to me about him often. It turned out that her story about their affair was quite different from his story. He had portrayed her as some kind of nympho who had thrown herself at him, and he'd gone along with it despite himself. In her version of events, she was sleeping regularly with R, and she seemed both happy and distressed. He was *difficult*, she said. Difficult because he was hot and cold with her too. One day he'd have sex with her and tell her they could only ever be casual, and another day he'd seduce her and say he wanted long-term commitment, and another day he didn't want to go to bed with her at all, and then she'd see him at a conference and he'd be mean to her.

I hadn't the heart to tell Chloë that I'd had a one-night stand with him. The possibility crossed my mind that perhaps he'd slept with me as a way of hurting her, and I wasn't going to allow our friendship to be degraded by a shitstorm of jealousy over a man trying to play us off against each other. So it remained my guilty secret, but when I listened to her speaking about him, I tried to encourage her to step back, to think about the way he was treating her.

I don't think she digested my advice at all. I could see that she was lost in a fog and she couldn't see clearly. While I could easily perceive *her* fog, I hadn't yet entirely perceived my own.

Chloë emphasized to me how 'important' R was in his profession. Indeed, he had more status, more money than her, more contacts. His power was a pull, but it intimidated her, blurred her boundaries of what was an acceptable way to be treated. I kept trying, gently, to convey that this didn't mean to say that she wasn't a person of equal status and value who deserved respect.

A comic interchange occurred at a bookshop event a few weeks later. There, I ended up chatting to R as we queued to get our books signed. I told R about a video I'd seen on YouTube, in which a famous alt-right speaker asserted to his female interviewer that 'only 7 per cent of women are feminists'. She looked unconvinced and repeated his statistic in a tone of doubt. I was about to elaborate that I believed that…

When R cut in and talked over me: 'Oh yeah, even if only 7 per cent of women are feminists, then it doesn't matter. The point is, feminist theory is sound, so we should all support it.'

I opened my mouth to interject that, actually, I had fact-checked the 2016 study I believed the alt-right speaker was referring to. It was commissioned by the Fawcett Society, and the results showed a much more complex picture. Only 7 per cent of Britons *call* themselves feminists – 9 per cent of women and 4 per cent of men. *But* 74 per cent of women said that they were sympathetic to feminism and equality between the sexes. It was the label 'feminism' that women did not like, some fearing it was 'bitchy' or misandrist. Furthermore, a 2018 YouGov poll found that 34 per cent of women said 'yes' when asked if they were a feminist (up from 27 per cent in 2013).

Before I could say this to R, he had spotted someone else he wanted to talk to and strolled off, and so to this day I wonder if he still believes the fallacy that only 7 per cent of British women are feminists.

# IV

I had heard the term 'gaslighting' many, many times by the time I'd met R, both in a personal and political context. The *Oxford English Dictionary* named gaslighting as one of their most popular words of 2018, and we have President Donald Trump to thank for that. According to Trump, reality is whatever you want it to be, and you can change it from minute to minute, whether you are citing the number of people at your inauguration compared to Obama's (even though photographic evidence suggests otherwise), or wielding a Sharpie to plot the fictional path of Hurricane Dorian so that it matches your public statement.

The term derives from the 1938 play *Gas Light* by Patrick Hamilton. An Oscar-winning film adaptation, starring Ingrid Bergman, was released in 1944. Bergman plays a woman called Paula Alquist who is seduced by Gregory Anton, played by Charles Boyer, marrying him after a whirlwind romance. Then life takes on a surreal slant. Pictures disappear from the walls of their home, and he persuades her that she took them; the absence of an heirloom brooch that he steals is deemed the fault of her carelessness. Paula asks why the gas lamps seem to flicker when he goes up into the attic, but he assures her that it is all in her mind. Gregory, it transpires, is a criminal hiding the sins of his past. He isolates Paula from the outside world until she becomes afraid of going out in public. He does all that he can to convince her that she is going mad, for if she is institutionalized, he can gain power of attorney.

Paula is saved by a chance meeting with a detective, who decides to investigate Gregory. In the final scene, she has her revenge. Gregory, facing arrest, is tied to a chair, and he attempts to manipulate Paula, pleading with her to cut him free. She taunts him by feigning madness, wielding a knife and questioning whether it is 'real', before calling the police to take him away.

Gaslighting has become so ubiquitous a term that some people argue it is losing its potency. Yet it did not occur to me that the word was applicable to my situation with R. In my head, I probably had a vague idea that it was a term for other women, weaker women, women who put up with male idiots and wankers.

Perhaps my ego was at stake: who wants to believe they're being made a fool of? Who wants to feel that a relationship, or a friendship, in which they experience sincere and genuine emotion, is a sham? In such a scenario, revelation becomes humiliation. Furthermore, being a full-time writer for many years has helped me to develop both a heightened sense of detachment and also empathy with a multiplicity of viewpoints. So I had empathy for R, a willingness to accept his assertions and engage with his viewpoint.

Gaslighters are obsessed with maintaining control and power. It is a process that tends to happen softly in a relationship, as gradual as a shift of season. A typical gaslighter is self-centred and low on empathy, drawn to his emotional opposite: someone who is conscientious and compassionate. At the start of a relationship, he might well idealize his partner, lavishing her with praise; then he will create a destabilizing vacuum by withdrawing affection, causing her to panic and wonder what she has done wrong. This is followed by games that are played out with spiderweb subtlety: criticizing, controlling, nitpicking, telling her what to wear, shaming her, isolating her from friends and family.

Another classic characteristic of a gaslighter is their ability to play hot and cold. This, too, distorts your sense of reality. When you're getting to know someone, you tend to learn a little bit about them each time you meet, which gradually coalesces into intimacy. With a gaslighter, that natural process is disturbed, as is an ability to perceive a clear-cut narrative of where your relationship is heading. In the resulting smaze, they then assert *this is what happened*, and it can become easier to believe their 'truth' rather than formulate a story from your own muddle. A friend of mine once told me about a womanizer he knew, whose successful strategy was predicated on keeping 'women in a constant state of disorientation'. One of the warning signs that you are dealing with a gaslighter is the constant nagging of whispers such as: *Am I being too sensitive? Am I good enough for my partner? Why am I always in the wrong, always apologizing?*

One of the most tragic elements of an abusive relationship is that a perpetrator will turn compassion into a vice, perceiving kindness as a crack that they can cleave open. Such humanity – the essence of empathy – should be cherished; but, sadly, compassion for a perpetrator equals compliance. It is precisely this propensity for warmth and goodwill that often ensnares a woman as much as fear does.

In 2017, Kai Cole, an architect and producer, wrote an open letter to *TheWrap* about her relationship with the film-maker Joss Whedon. After sixteen years of marriage, they had agreed to divorce. He had been having numerous affairs, and while this is neither a shocking nor unusual reason for a relationship to end, Cole was devastated by the years she had spent being deceived and doubting her own instincts. Whedon, the writer-director of *Buffy the Vampire Slayer* and numerous films which featured strong female heroines, had previously been honoured with a feminist award from Equality Now as one of the 'men on the front lines' of their cause. Cole asserted that Whedon had admitted that he was a man who 'lived two lives' during their marriage, though his official response to the piece was a statement from his spokesperson: 'While this account includes inaccuracies and misrepresentations which can be harmful to their family, Joss is not commenting, out of concern for his children and out of respect for his ex-wife.'

Cole wrote that her husband 'never conceded the hypocrisy of being out in the world preaching feminist ideals, while at the same time, taking away my right to make choices for my life and my body based on the truth'. And: 'I believed, everyone believed, that he was one of the good guys, committed to fighting for women's rights, committed to our marriage, and to the women he worked with. But I now see how he used his relationship with me as a shield, both during and after our marriage, so no one would question his relationships with other women or scrutinize his writing as anything other than feminist.'

Women can be gaslighters, too. While researching this essay, I met men who had been devastated by socio-pathic women who had wrecked their lives through relationships or the workplace. One man I interviewed, who suffered years of emotional torture from a female narcissist, confided: 'Although the experience was pain-ful, I do feel that when men go through this, it is less likely to affect their careers', but another told me the tale of a female gaslighter at a publishing company who had managed to get three colleagues fired through her manipulations. It would be wrong to attribute this vice to one sex. Gaslighting is not a trait that anyone inherits or is born with, but a social skill that the perpetrator observes and mimics and refines over a period of time.

However, therapist Robin Stern – having treated thousands of couples – argues that women are more prone to becoming ensnared by gaslighters because they 'are socialized to doubt themselves and continually apologize for disagreeing with or upsetting their partners'.

· Perhaps, too, women are more susceptible to being persuaded that they're 'mad' and more nervous of the term's connotations. In the Victorian era, eccentricity was a quality that was celebrated in men, while female madness was frequently labelled 'hysteria', a word which has its roots in the Greek *hystera*, meaning uterus, for the illness was thought to be caused by a defect in the womb.

One evening in late 2016 I watched actor Claire Foy being interviewed by Graham Norton. She described how she had filmed *The Crown* while nursing her newborn baby, which meant that she had to breastfeed between takes. 'I was lunatic,' she said, 'I was mad…' even though it was clear that she was far from it: she was lucid, intelligent, witty, dynamic, and the word 'mad' was just a flippant term of self-deprecation. After that, I noticed how frequently I heard women using the term as a way of doing themselves down. I was queuing to buy a coffee in a café; two women were in front of me, and one of them kept changing her mind about which piece of cake she was going to buy. 'Don't worry, I'm totally mad,' she said cheerfully. It is a hyperbolic way of saying *forgive me*, when no forgiveness is really due. It is a term which immediately makes a woman likeable.

Perhaps it is a reflection of a society where women were once more likely to end up in asylums and are now more likely to be on antidepressants. In the US, women are twice as likely to take them as men. Given that suicide rates are far higher for men than women, it may be the case that women have a greater tendency to take pills for depression because they are more prone to reporting their worries about their mental health. Women grow up in a society that judges whether or not they are fit mothers, through the media and social services and the medical powers; there is an insidious pressure for them to be 'sane' and behave in a conformist manner. Furthermore, when women go to the doctor, they are more likely to be prescribed antidepressants even when they don't need them, while the reverse is true for men, whose depression is more likely to be underdetected and undertreated.

Or, another argument goes, it might reflect the way that men and women are socialized to handle stress. Men are often conditioned from an early age to be stoic; they are not encouraged to develop the emotional literacy to share what they are feeling. Men direct their negative emotions into anger and aggression, while women

ruminate on their depression and amplify it. Men tend
to go to the pub to drown their sorrows; women smother
them with pills washed down with water. Men direct
their stress outwards, women inwards. It is less shameful
for a woman to cry than a man, and a female drunk is
still more frowned upon than a male one. Daniel Nettle
makes the point that when 'the numbers of men who
are alcoholic or impulsively violent are added to the
numbers who are depressed the total is about the same
as the number of women who are depressed'. And he
observes that in the Old Order Amish community, where
there is no substance abuse and crime rates are nearly
zero, men get depressed just as commonly as women.

The idea that women who are 'vulnerable' are more
prone to attracting an abusive relationship is misguided.
A self-confessed gaslighter, a Canadian lawyer called
Greg, gave an interview for the BBC where he related
how he would cheat on the women he dated. Gaslighting
was his key weapon in maintaining a double life; he dis-
tracted one partner from trace evidence of his infidelity
on social media by shaming her that she spent too much
time online and gradually convincing her that she was
'crazy', 'paranoid' and 'full of drama'.

The psychologist George K. Simon says that there
are two key traits that attract gaslighters: 'conscientiousness' and 'agreeableness'. But Greg added a few more:
intelligent, successful women. He explained that such
women usually have a strong idea of what sort of man

they want. Because he could clearly perceive the romantic narrative that they were seeking, it became easy to play to that storyline and then distort it. He argued that 'from my experience, it's not true that it is vulnerable or insecure women who are susceptible to gaslighting'. This is why such relationships can go on for so long: those who are being gaslit may also be invested in the fantasy of their relationship, and, as they are weakened by their partners, they cling to the idea that everything is fine and that their loved one is perfect.

Most accounts of gaslighting online involve similar images – men who 'get under their partner's skin' and men who 'get into their partner's head' as though their psychological domination is akin to a virus that, once caught, becomes parasitic in nature. Ultimately, the experience of being gaslit or abused involves a dissolution of the self. One victim who escaped from such a relationship, Kay Schubach, observed that it is 'very, very common' that 'your self-esteem gets eroded. In my case, that happened very quickly but sometimes it's a long, slow erosion. I've seen incredibly strong, beautiful, forthright women… disintegrate into a shell of themselves. They don't even know who they are anymore. They have trouble getting out of the house, they have trouble putting on makeup, getting dressed. They've just lost all sense of themselves.'

# V

On average, a woman in a bad relationship will endure fifty instances of abuse, emotional or physical, before she receives effective help. But withdrawing from an abuser, or cutting them out of your life, is often a moment fraught with danger: 50 to 75 per cent of domestic violence murders occur at the point of break-up or after she has left her abuser.

The moment I pulled away from R, the moment I woke up and realized that flirting with him was an act of masochism, that our game would always end in me losing, was a pivot on which our friendship turned. I mentioned to R that I had gone on a date and kissed another man. I thought it would make no difference to him; he was, after all, sleeping with numerous other women. But R seemed to intuit that he had lost his hold over me.

I remember the moment clearly: I saw R at a social event, and he had his back to me. I went up to him, tapped him on the shoulder. When he turned to face me, his expression was one of complete and utter disgust and fury. I remember recoiling, utterly taken aback, as he quickly forced his grimace into a smile. An hour later, I was chatting to a woman and he bounced up to us and joined in the conversation with warmth and wit. I thought: how weird, his hot and cold behaviour is no longer alternating between one occasion and another but taking place all within the space of one evening. Perhaps another reason for his public show of niceness was the importance of maintaining an alibi at a time when #MeToo was changing the world around him: *You've seen me be pleasant to Sam, so if she ever tells anyone about my behaviour, how can any of it be true?*

A few weeks on, he sent a cartoon to me – for intended publication online – about a character with my name. R had artistic skill, and he could draw well. In the strip of pictures, 'Sam' was portrayed as a slutty writer with a poor prose style. It was a crafted piece of satire where his hatred bittered every pencil stroke. I did not react. I figured that he was sleeping with so many women it was likely he had copulated with dozens of Sams, any of whom might have been a target; or perhaps we had all coalesced into one epitome of femininity at which he was directing his fury. It never got published, but I looked at it incessantly and felt the sting of it as if others were looking at it too.

Why, I wondered, was he so angry with me when he had so many other women in his harem? A friend of mine thought that R wanted to feel that I was there, dangling, ready and willing to sleep with him *should* he choose to. He wanted to be in control. The one who rejected, but was not subject to rejection himself.

Chloë, who was still engaged in an ongoing on–off romance with him, told me how highly R was regarded by his female friends, how he was in demand as a speaker at international conferences. And so I remained convinced that my problem was unique to me, a private struggle that I was to blame for in some way I could not fathom.

A few weeks later, I attended another gathering at an art gallery where R was present; he had brought along a friend from academia. Halfway through the night, I went to the toilet and noticed a young woman at the sink. Her eyes were glassy with melancholy, her forced smile like someone trying to prop up a wilting flower in a vase. I chatted to her briefly, but I could see that she wasn't in the mood for conversation. Shortly afterwards, she went home. Her sorrow left an afterburn; I worried about her, hoped she was okay.

Then R's friend enlightened me. The woman, he gossiped, had slept with R. She'd come to the party hoping for something more, and R had told her where to go. Meanwhile, R was sitting in a group of people, laughing and chatting, indifferent to the woman's suffering. At this point, I was still making some excuses for R. I considered that relationships were tricky things. Cross-purposes were inevitable. I had no idea of the details of R's liaison. For all I knew, he might have been completely honest with her and she had harboured unrealistic expectations. I thought, *It's important not to be quick to judge, not to conflate my experience with her experience, to consider all sides of the story and accept my own ignorance.*

At the same time, I experienced a fleeting sense of guilty consolation that I was not the only woman who had had a difficult time with R.

What a relief it was to think: *It's not just me.*

It was a tool Weinstein used during his years of abuse: isolating his victims. He would gag them by getting them to sign non-disclosure agreements, throw cash at them and intimidate them into remaining silent. We have the full picture now, but at the time all the women had were pieces of a puzzle, not knowing how their piece fitted, not knowing if they were alone in their bad experience, feeling lost and powerless. When Weinstein was close to being brought down, he became particularly anxious about Gwyneth Paltrow outing him. She was, in fact, having regular conversations with the *New York Times*. As though sensing how precarious his situation was becoming, he would call her often and ask for assurance that she was not betraying him. Later, Paltrow found out that he used her as a gaslighting tool:

he lied to young actresses that she had slept with him on the basis that they could have a career like hers if they gave in to him.

The #MeToo movement gave me perspective on my situation – or so I thought. I told myself that I was lucky. I had not encountered a monster like Weinstein. I had slept with someone who had turned out to be a bit of a prick, but our sex had been consensual, and though I had suffered a bit of nasty behaviour, I would survive it. I hadn't suffered from a long-term cycle of abuse which might have threatened my sanity.

I thought to myself: *The world is full of unpleasant people, and from time to time you brush up against one.* I recalled the advice of a publisher: 'The best way to proceed in your career in the literary world is just be nice to people. If someone is mean or unpleasant, just ignore them, hold your head high and move on.' (The publisher was female and she had spoken to a female audience who had smiled in obedient acquiescence.) It didn't occur to me then that there might be any real ramifications. At that point in time, the idea would have been ludicrous.

*After all*, I thought, *he chased me.* He'd initiated the sex; he'd specified that he wanted no more than that, and so why the hell would he have any reason to give me a hard time?

And, indeed, just before the house of cards collapsed, R and I seemed to have finally reached a good place.

We exchanged warm, jokey emails; we met at a party and had a playful, friendly chat. His bad behaviour was forgotten. All seemed well.

R was drunk that night, and he seemed in a bitter mood. It was a lively social event in the arts world, in which I was enjoying meeting people and having a good time. In particular, I connected with a young playwright who was interested in potentially adapting my book for the stage. R watched us chatting with dark eyes. I couldn't work out why he was so pissed off. Then I realized that he thought I was trying to seduce the guy.

A few hours earlier, R had confided in me, over drinks, that he had slept with dozens of women during his summer in the UK. He'd thought that being away from home would be liberating. Instead, the experience had filled him with self-disgust. I looked at him and suddenly had a Wizard of Oz moment. I had pulled back the curtain and realized that he was not a charismatic cad but possibly a sex addict. It struck me that he was desperately in need of help, with little recognition of his problem, because he had grown up in a society that had told him he was a real man, that to conquer and seduce was a victory. I'd been told by a friend that he wanted love, marriage, kids, but that his divorce had made him feel it would never work out for him. Now I had an insight as to why.

R began mansplaining to me under the guise of giving me 'advice'. Despite the fact that he had only ever written academic texts, he felt that he needed to educate me. The title of my forthcoming memoir, he informed me, was clichéd and boring. My name sounded too working-class. He kept on picking at me, putting me down. We argued about a spat on Twitter between a well-known female writer and her ex, and he expressed his anger that various women had sided with her and tweeted things such as their hatred of the patriarchy in consolation. 'Imagine if a woman did that to me!' he said, and I sensed a fear lurking beneath his anger. It was related to a general unease I witnessed around him that summer: the shock of #MeToo, of societal values shifting around him, of whether his own behaviour to women was still viable, if he might be judged by friends or colleagues.

Towards the end of the evening, he disappeared for a while and then re-entered with the playwright. R glared at me coldly. The playwright, previously so friendly, frowned at me and left without saying goodbye. I found out later (some months on) that R had been slating me to him.

I had nightmares that night. I realized that if R carried on like this, he could perhaps wreak considerable damage on my career.

Fear became a backdrop to my life. I was plagued by whispers of worry. Who else might he be speaking to? Finally, R had achieved the ultimate aim of any gaslighter: he had got under my skin and into my head.

I've had many troubling and difficult experiences of assault during my lifetime, as most women have. I've walked down an alleyway and seen a man flash at me. I've sat on a Tube next to a drunk man and been groped by him and had to fend him off. I've suffered a minor sexual assault. I've endured one toxic relationship where, in its final breaking-down phase, on one sole occasion, my partner hit me. But none of these made a lasting mark on me – which is not to trivialize these experiences and the long-term damage they can inflict – and I was able to move on relatively quickly without being scarred by them. My encounters with R felt a hundred times worse than any of these experiences, yet I could not claim that he had laid a finger on me: it was all psychological, subtle, insidious. And, therefore, very difficult to explain to anyone.

*How*, I wondered, *am I going to resolve this?*

# VI

Here is the transcript of a successful woman I interviewed called B. She is in her early thirties, works in the arts and describes her experience with a chauvo-feminist:

> X was a powerful man, an arts editor on a mainstream magazine. I was living abroad and making a living as a writer. I met him for a drink at a cocktail bar and he was flirtatious, especially given that he knew I had a boyfriend. I wasn't upset or bothered by him flirting; at the end of the night, I took a cab home alone.
>
> A month later, I found myself at a low ebb. I was anxious about a book coming out. My boyfriend had gone back to the US; our relationship was over; I had a few more days in the country before I headed back to the UK. X got in touch and asked to meet up again, so I agreed to go for a drink with him. When I texted him to say that I was running late,

he replied *okay, good girl*, to which I replied, *Are we in an episode of* Mad Men? His return was, *Sorry, I got carried away*. During our drink, he spoke about a woman he was seeing who was in New York and then said, 'So I really shouldn't be on a date like this!' And I thought, *God, no, this isn't a date*.

But at the end of the night, he kissed me, and I decided to go back to his place. Back at his flat, he started kissing me, and suddenly he had a complete change of personality. He had always seemed pleasant and charming; now he became very aggressive and violent. He began to pull my hair and pinch me and bite me. I said, 'I'm really not into that. Stop,' and he eventually stopped, saying he had a girlfriend in the US anyway. But even then he started being nasty. He told me: 'I know what you're like now,' implying that I was some kind of slut. I said to him, 'Do you do that to all women?' and he said yes. I asked him if he was a sadist and to what extent he liked to physically hurt women, and he replied, 'I like to hurt women until they cry.' I was disturbed and keen to head home.

Outside on the street, he flagged me a cab. I went to give him a hug, and he said, 'What the fuck is this?' He kissed me aggressively, groping me under my clothes, then opened the cab door, shoved me in next to the driver and said, 'Humiliated?' The driver smirked. The whole charade had been played out for the driver's amusement too – he had seen it all, the kiss, the groping, the game. The next morning, I saw bruises on my arms from the way he had pinched me.

When I was back in the UK, however, we exchanged a few friendly DMs. A few years later, I saw him tweeting a link to a lengthy magazine piece he had written about Harvey Weinstein. He argued that life was going to improve greatly for female actors now that men like Weinstein were being outed, and what a wonderful thing that was.

In the hysterical backlash against the #MeToo movement, one argument that was often cited was the idea that the scandal reinforced gender clichés.

Suddenly all these powerful men were predatory wolves and women were lambs to the slaughter. Camille Paglia, writing for the *Hollywood Reporter*, argued that the #MeToo movement is 'taking us back to the Victorian archetypes of early silent films, where twirling villains tied damsels in distress to railroad tracks'. Germaine Greer said it was encouraging 'victim culture'. Melanie Phillips, writing in *The Times*, argued that: 'Female emancipation was all about giving women control over their own destinies. Now they have that control, they are presenting themselves once again as powerless victims of male oppression, even whilst benefiting from being presented as sex objects.'

But it is too simplistic to couch the experiences of women in these terms. The women who came up against Weinstein reacted in a variety of ways, both passive and aggressive. Some tried to fight back, without much success. Lauren O'Connor wrote a memo reporting on the 'toxic environment for women' at Miramax, which she sent to HR. Once the memo was sent, she was asked not to come back to the office and was offered an NDA for her exit and silence. Salma Hayek refused to give in to Weinstein's demands for massages and sex, but the result was that Weinstein spent years cajoling her or flying into rages; on one occasion, he threatened to kill her. He also sought to crush her film project (*Frida*), and it was only her formidable willpower and dynamism that enabled her to push the project through – though not without being degraded from actress to porn star, forced to film an unnecessary lesbian sex scene which was not even in the script. Hayek, aware that she was filming purely for Weinstein's private titillation, threw up beforehand, found herself 'convulsing and crying' and had to take a tranquillizer to get through the scene.

Yet it is true that a number of the women who found themselves in Weinstein's hotel suite reacted by freezing up. In theory, in an ideal world, his victims ought to have been 'empowered' enough to act like the badass heroine in a movie, kick him in the balls and storm out. (Not that the power dynamics of Miramax would have allowed them to be the victor even if they had done that. Judging from his past patterns of behaviour, it is likely that Weinstein would not have interpreted such an encounter as being put in his place; he would have just had them 'let go' from the company.)

This ideal of female empowerment shows a lack of understanding as to how trauma affects the psyche – the paralysis and dissociation it can invoke. As the actress Paz de la Huerta remarks in *Untouchable*, 'when you read about rape, the girl kicks and screams but that's not exactly right'. And Hope D'Amore, reacting to Weinstein's huge physical bulk and strength, as well as his psychological bullying – 'Do you really want to make an enemy out of me for five minutes of your time?' – found herself saying no but not 'scratching out his eyes', feeling that 'I thought if I just shut up, it'd be over in five minutes.'

It's a common biological response to rape or assault: the body freezes up in shock; the victim goes limp. Yet it is one that is often not taken into account by the law; three-quarters of European states recognize an assault only when physical violence, threats or coercion are involved.

When I interviewed women who had found them-selves in unasked-for, ambiguous sexual situations with men, I found echoes: they did not act as masters of their destiny but with physical passivity, mental confusion and numbness. Yet these women were not passive in nature. They were spirited, smart, sharp. They were successful in their careers. These reports may make us uncomfortable because they don't fit in with our ideas of female empowerment in our society. Rather than scorning such testimonials, it is worth examining and unpicking why victims might react in such a way.

I thought back to the first sexual violation I ever experienced. I was travelling from Oxford to London on the coach. It was winter, the outside world a blur of darkness, the window pure reflection. I watched my face staring back at me, pale and anxious; the person sitting next to me had put their hand up my skirt and was circling their fingertips against my thigh. I froze up. I was terrified that if I moved an inch they might pull a knife on me. For the next hour, it went on and on. I was locked into the terror of present discomfort and anticipation of worse to come. When the journey ended, I feared, I would be followed and raped. As the coach rolled up at Victoria and they got off, I saw them waiting by the hatch for their bags, watching me with hawk eyes. Their hair was short, their features feminine; in the blur of shock, I could not tell if they were man or woman. I fled. They did not come after me.

I had another bad experience at the age of thirty. On a trip to India, staying at an Ayurveda clinic, I made friends with a young doctor there. One day he asked to come into my bedroom for some kind of 'Jyotish' analysis which would involve him examining 'the width of my palm' as some kind of indication of personality and destiny. He then started trying to 'measure' my breasts, and when I pushed him away he carried on groping me. I was uncomfortable, but it took far too long for me to eventually tell him to leave. I was not traumatized by the encounter, but I was certainly pissed off. I kept him at a distance for the rest of my stay there.

When I analyse it, I am concerned by my own behaviour as much as that of the man in question: why didn't I just tell him to leave the moment he transgressed? It's not as though I was turned on in any way; I was merely disgusted. Why didn't I act as I once did when I was on a train and a drunken man sitting next to me put his hand on my leg? On that occasion, I slapped his hand away and glared at him and he was cowed.

I think that knowing the doctor complicated my response to his behaviour. It wasn't as black and white a scenario as a stranger on a train, where I had a clear-cut enemy. I had been getting on well with the doctor, who was charming and handsome; I was anxious that by agreeing to let him into my room I had somehow invited his behaviour.

*Why didn't they just leave?* It's a question that has been asked time and time again as more #MeToo stories have been shared. When Louis C.K. cornered women and masturbated in front of them, why didn't they just walk out? We can see this echoed in responses to the Aziz Ansari scandal. Various sarcastic articles about the encounter questioned, *Why didn't she just call her herself a cab?* Why did she go along with it? Why did she give him a blow job? Where was her *agency?* Part of the misunderstanding between them resulted from Ansari failing to listen and observe, but then neither did Grace assert herself strongly enough. Some of her mental paralysis, it seems, came from the confusion of Ansari's chauvo-feminism. Having seen his shows and read excerpts from his dating guide, *Modern Romance*, she wasn't expecting this sort of behaviour from him.

I thought, too, of the girls' high school I attended, where my female friends and I had sometimes found ourselves in uneasy situations with boys who had gone too far. Yet I cast my mind back to any sports session, and I remember that it was complete carnage. We would transform from nice, pleasant, smiling girls in skirts to monsters wielding hockey sticks, shoving each other in netball, our elbows weapons, competing with playful violence. Nobody watching us on those pitches could come to the clichéd biological conclusion that while men are competitive predators, women are innately docile. Despite the fact that we were happy to bruise each other on the pitch, when it came to men with unwanted hands on our bodies, we sometimes found ourselves numb and mute and confused.

Was it an issue of education? Socialization? I thought back to my own upbringing and education, of how I had been encouraged by my mother to actively pursue a career in writing because I had shown an aptitude and passion for it. My teachers had warned me that it was unlikely I would get into Oxford, which had simply spurred me on to work twice as hard to prove that I could. Getting published had involved years of rejection, but I had pushed through with fierce resolve. I had been taught to be dynamic in my career; I had been the co-director of a publishing company; I had demonstrated strength and determination – so why the hell had I found myself in these uncomfortable situations with men? Why had I carried on having sex with R even when he told me about sleeping with a friend of mine while his cock was inside me? Why had I allowed the doctor in India to casually grope me?

At school, we weren't properly educated on these thorny issues. The only advice that I can remember being given was from a visiting lecturer who counselled us on things you might say to deter a rapist. The theoretical 'rapists' were always virtual demons: men armed with knives, hiding in shadows and bushes, dragging women into dirty alleyways. In reality, eight out of ten assaults and rapes occur with men that women already know and involve far more complex scenarios and grey areas.

If anything, #MeToo was an admission that in sexual situations our recourse to power was not as clear-cut and immediate as we'd thought. But the honest recognition of that *is* empowering. An awareness of it can help future generations of women to feel they can call that cab, they can say no, they can speak up.

B, for example, came to this conclusion:

Since the #MeToo movement, my attitude has changed. When I was at X's flat, I didn't realize how inappropriate, violating and disrespectful his sexual behaviour was. I thought because I had gone back to his flat I had at least partially consented to it. And I would have thought the same of other women in similar situations. #MeToo has made me more aware that women have the right to assert their boundaries wherever and whenever – and when someone transgresses these boundaries, there's no 'grey area'. They are clearly in the wrong.

# VII

Just as B felt that she had been empowered by #MeToo, I also felt inspired to stand up to R. Had his abuse occurred a decade ago, even a few years ago, perhaps he would have kept on and on undermining me, but I felt a stronger sense of agency. I believed that I had the power to fight back.

But the question still bothered me as to what to do.

It still vexed me that I had not been able to resolve the situation through being pleasant and polite to R. Perhaps the worst myth that I had absorbed from growing up with romances and fairy tales is the fallacy that women can civilize men. A good relationship will help both parties to nourish and grow, but there can be a wrongful emphasis on the woman's duty to perform a sort of alchemy on her partner. It's the old story of the bad guy and the innocent virgin; it's the tale of *Les Liaisons Dangereuses* and *Grease* and a thousand other stories where a woman tames and humanizes and heals a bad guy.

As a writer, I have been to numerous storytelling and screenwriting classes which teach the concept of a *character arc*, that key transformation of character that occurs as a protagonist reacts to conflict and makes choices. Any good movie, we were taught, must involve a fundamental shift in the character's psychology. A geeky young man is bitten by a spider and becomes a superhero; a young cop takes on a Goliath of a villain and brings him to justice. The arc constitutes a redemptive path from innocence to experience, from weakness to strength. In real life, we rarely change with such sharp shifts of gear. I do believe that we eventually learn from our mistakes, but often after repeating them a dozen-odd times, for life wisdom is something we acquire terribly slowly. Hollywood character arcs contain a compression of time, decades of learning speeded up into one brief window in a character's life.

While many relationships do result in growth for both sexes, when you're dealing with an abuser your good behaviour will make little difference. You cannot be the facilitator of their redemption. It is hard to digest that even in the depths of the most intimate relationship their abuse has very little to do with you; it is being inflicted *on* you and, as such, has a strangely impersonal quality.

What to do? Increasingly, my situation with R felt like a catch-22: if I maintained a pleasant, polite attitude, it would be interpreted as an invitation for him to carry on, but if I stood up to him I feared that he would simply gaslight me, or else become inflamed and retaliate.

When you decide to stand up to an abuser, you are also faced with the challenge of the social circle around you, the wider issue of the society you live in. It is not always easy to neatly carve that person out of your life.

Women can become trapped in a cage of doubt. One of the post-#MeToo myths is that the women who spoke out were all desperate to share their stories in their eagerness to get 'attention'. In fact, it took months and years for the investigative journalists to hunt down Weinstein's victims, and, to begin with, they had no idea of the scale of his abuse. Many had signed agreements that gagged them. Many ignored calls, felt anxious about coming out, fretted about the effect on their careers; all had to be cajoled. We can see what a seismic shift #MeToo was when we consider that the staff at the *New York Times* had no idea how people would react to the piece, or indeed if anyone would care. Ronan Farrow found there was a lack of support for airing the story from his employers at NBC and so ended up taking it to the *New Yorker* instead.

When the New York Attorney General Eric Schneiderman was slapping and shaming his girlfriends in private, they had doubts about coming forward. They were nervous, uncertain, edgy. Michelle Manning Barish explained: 'I was ashamed. For victims, shame played a huge role in most of these stories.' Another girlfriend who was slapped by him explained the social pressures of speaking out against a man who was powerful and successful: 'A number of them advised her to keep the story to herself, arguing that Schneiderman was too valuable a politician for the Democrats to lose.'

This is the paradox of gaslighters and abusers: they may have a nice side. They may be doing good in the world as well as bad. When Eric Schneiderman was finally brought down, his ex-wife, Jennifer Cunningham, said that she found it impossible to believe the allegations because she had known Eric for nearly thirty-five years as a husband, father and friend: 'These allegations are completely inconsistent with the man I know, who has always been someone of the highest character, outstanding values and a loving father.'

We like to caricature and villainize abusive men. In the *Untouchable* documentary about Weinstein, a very common epithet used to describe him is 'charming', and, indeed, one of his male colleagues spoke about having 'survivor guilt': his time working with Weinstein was rewarding and enriching. One of the hardest things to stomach about an abuser is that their behaviour is like a coin toss. Heads: they are nice, kind, decent, funny, helpful, charming. Tails: they can be vindictive, vile, controlling and gaslighting. This is exactly why abusers get away with it: because these contradictions confuse the people around them. This was the case for me and R, too. An array of male and female friends and colleagues experienced the best of him; the women he'd slept with experienced the worst.

We're brought up in a society where revenge narratives are one of our most popular universal stories. Cinderella, for example, avenges herself on the Ugly Sisters and gets her Prince Charming. Hollywood movies love to posit a good guy who achieves pure justice against the bad guy, triumphantly nullifying him in Act Three. Revenge stories usually end in happily-ever-afters. In real life, achieving justice against someone who has wronged you can be a miserable affair, one without a neat ending, and involving a messy aftermath. When considering whether to stand up to an abuser, you can end up like Hamlet, locked in endless internal debates of self-doubt.

The popularity of the revenge narrative also feeds into the myth that women who come forward to speak out, to name and shame perpetrators, stand to gain from the experience. The idea is that they get some kind of glory from being victims, that they get fame, money, sympathy. In fact, the reality is often the reverse. They may lose friends, money, time, energy, status. In a 2019 article for *The Cut*, a number of women and men spoke about the aftermath of coming forward.

The article, written by Rebecca Traister, made the point that many of the men who were disgraced were seen as complex villains, the media keen to portray them as tragic anti-heroes suffering a fall from grace, while their accusers were often caricatured as being part of a mob. She asks the key question: what about their contradictions and complexities? What about how their lives have been affected? Many, she noted, found that getting hired again after going public about harassment could be a significant hurdle. Stress, nightmares, sickness were a norm. Christine Blasey Ford had to move house four times due to death threats; she has to pay for private security and is yet to return to her job as a professor at Palo Alto University. Many had to suffer huge legal bills; Rose McGowan, in order to fund her legal fees against Weinstein, had to sell her house. Christie Van, who complained about harassment at the Ford Motor Company, found that she suffered retaliation rather than being offered support. She was assaulted in the car park after work, pushed to the ground and accused for being 'a black snitch bitch'; her attacker threatened to kill her if she returned. Having left work, she suffered homelessness. She concluded, 'I would never do it again and I would never recommend another woman do it.' Ford's reaction to her claims was: 'Ford does not tolerate sexual harassment or discrimination', though the company did eventually settle in court.

Traister compares these women to front-line soldiers who have often been sacrificed for a greater long-term movement for positive change.

Some of Weinstein's accusers – had Weinstein not had the power to pick up the phone and bad-mouth them, effectively stalling their progress – could have gone on to flourish as great actresses. They might have won Oscars, made millions. Instead, they became defined as the women who brought down Weinstein, effectively becoming supporting acts in his monstrous narrative.

It wasn't easy for the actresses abused by Weinstein to speak out. It is even harder for women in low-paid jobs, who may be terrified of coming forward because they can't afford to run the risk of losing their salary. Women from BAME backgrounds are more likely to suffer harassment. They are over-represented in industries such as hospitality, health, food services and retail – the very industries where there are the greatest numbers of sexual-harassment claims. A woman on a zero-hours contract may find she does not have any protections; and women who are undocumented immigrants are also particularly vulnerable, with no recourse at all.

In the UK, the coalition government abolished Section 40 of the Equality Act in 2013 in order to get rid of 'red tape' in businesses. The Act meant employers had to take 'reasonable steps' to ensure their workforce was protected from sexual harassment by a third party, such as customers or patients. A piece in the *New Statesman* illustrates a consequence, citing the case of Caitie, a woman who worked at a stand in a shopping centre in Glasgow. A man who followed her to work masturbating started turning up at her workplace, but she was told by her employers that he was a 'welcome shopper'. As Sarah Ditum points out, 'what the government actually cut were women's rights'.

# VIII

A few friends of mine, having observed the dynamic between R and me, asked, 'Don't you ever feel tempted to out him on Twitter?'

My answer was always no. I did not feel comfortable about doing so. For one thing, I had not been assaulted physically, so I reasoned that it did not count as a #MeToo story. Furthermore, how was I supposed to convey the subtleties of emotional abuse in a series of tweets consisting of 280 characters? Even an article would not suffice. I imagined possible smears. I pictured R dredging up any positive emails we'd exchanged and saying, 'Ha! She joked with me, she! She liked me!' I dreaded the thought of forcing our group of mutual acquaintances to divide and take sides. I dreaded the thought that while a number of people would be sympathetic, many would inevitably disbelieve me. I had been gaslit enough by R, and I could not stomach the thought of experiencing a wider, more public echo of that trauma. I would have no control over how people responded. Nor did I necessarily want to subject R to a braying, wrathful mob. I wanted to settle it in private.

I thought of a woman I knew who had the courage to tweet about a man who had harassed her. She did receive some online support and solidarity, but all throughout that week I heard people discussing it. Was she right to say something? Mostly, I heard people analysing *her* rather than *him*. That she was seeking attention, that there were attractive pics of her on her timeline, that she could not be trusted. I thought of my friend, B, who had declared that she had not wanted to out her chauvo-feminist because she feared it would define her.

There is a powerful scene in the second series of *Succession* which captures this predicament perfectly. The TV drama centres on the Roy family, who control the biggest media–entertainment company in the world. The family's empire is under threat, due to scandals from the past emerging, including sexual-harassment cases. Shiv – the daughter of the media mogul – is sent to persuade one victim to stay silent. Her compelling argument is that if she speaks out it will be 'the first and last line of your obituary'.

No, I thought, the Court of Twitter was not for me.

But I can see how and why trial by Twitter has evolved over the past decade. When Tarana Burke first created her #MeToo movement, 'Our vision from the beginning was to address both the dearth in resources for survivors of sexual violence and to build a community of advocates, driven by survivors, who will be at the forefront of creating solutions to interrupt sexual violence in their communities.'

The lack of justice in the courts has led to the internet being used as a substitute courtroom, where anonymous thousands act as jurors and hashtags become sentences of shame. This is not a fair way to dispense justice, but the weaknesses in the justice system, coupled with poor public attitudes towards rape, are the cause of it. Prior to #MeToo, many victims felt that nobody was interested in listening. Rose McGowan is constantly asked why it took her twenty years to come forward, to which she constantly answers, with grace and patience, that she did come forward twenty years ago – and nobody wanted to know. Molly Ringwald, in an article for the *New Yorker*, details how she was exploited and demeaned as a young actress but didn't feel she could complain because 'Stories like these have never been taken seriously. Women are shamed, told they are uptight, nasty, bitter, can't take a joke, are too sensitive. And the men? Well, if they're lucky, they might get elected President.' Lauren O'Connor, who wrote her brilliant memo about the toxic environment for women at Miramax, reflects on what happened to her: 'What I'm angry about is that there isn't another way. There isn't a system in place. You speak up through localized channels, such as HR, and nothing is done.

And nobody listens. And the only other avenue I've come to know is the press, which means mass exposure.'

The non-disclosure agreements (NDAs) that many of Weinstein's victims signed were a reflection of how assault was not taken seriously. Zelda Perkins, his former assistant, sought legal advice when Weinstein harassed her and allegedly raped a female colleague, Rowena Chiu. She wanted to go to court. But, 'I was told that wasn't even worth considering because of the disparity of power.' When she suggested she should go to Disney, the parent company of Miramax, whom she thought would be horrified, 'my naïvety was met with hilarity' by her lawyers. The NDAs, then, also became a shoddy substitute for conviction, and enabled male abusers to carry on controlling their victims through silencing them. Perkins was banned from even talking to a doctor about events unless they signed an NDA; Chiu felt unable to approach a trauma counsellor to discuss the rape she'd endured. She suffered depression, attempted suicide and did not even tell her husband what had happened to her. Perkins also found it hard to get work in the film industry because the gagging meant she was unable to tell anyone why she had left the company. While she struggled to repair her career, Weinstein carried on signing NDA after NDA, none of which clearly made any impact on his alleged behaviour but became a way of signing away his sins, enabling him to continue repeat-offending.

We live in a society in which rape is rarely punished. Many victims do not report rape or assault because the process is so harrowing. In 2015, Ambra Gutierrez reported Weinstein to the police and even obtained wiretap evidence, but no charges were made, and she was smeared in the press, painted as an opportunist and a prostitute. Chanel Miller was sexually assaulted behind a dumpster at a Stanford University fraternity party by Brock Turner when she was a student. In court, she had to endure pictures of her naked body being made public. She was painted a liar and a drunk. She found the process painful: 'When you're on the stand, you feel totally stripped and exposed. It didn't feel like we were working to get closer to the truth. It felt like a game of how quickly I could answer questions, if I could untangle the sentences the defense attorney was asking.' Having told her story, she was infuriated by the focus on how Brock's career as a competitive swimmer might be affected. He was convicted for just six months; after three, he was let out for 'good behaviour'.

The proportion of rapes prosecuted in England and Wales fell in December 2019 to 1.4 per cent. This compares to 7.4 per cent prosecution rates for crimes in general in that time period.

The reasons for this? A decade of austerity has certainly made an impact. There is a crisis in the British criminal-justice system caused by cuts to police funding and rising crime rates in general.

Most rapes and assaults are not reported. Only 15 per cent of those who have experienced sexual violence report it to the police. And yet it is widespread, for 20 per cent of women and 4 per cent of men have experienced some type of sexual assault after the age of sixteen. Approximately 90 per cent of those who have been raped knew the perpetrator prior to the offence. The Director of Public Prosecutions has stated that false rape allegations are 'serious but rare', constituting only 3 to 4 per cent of claims.

The average adult man in England and Wales is more likely to be raped than to be falsely accused of rape; for the former, his chances are 0.03 per cent; for the latter, 0.00021281 per cent.

In the US, there is an ongoing issue with hundreds of thousands of rape kits sitting untested in police departments and crime-lab storage facilities. Each kit is put together by a medical team and might include samples of bodily fluids, key for DNA testing. They lie neglected in part due to lack of funding – it costs between $1,000 and $1,500 to process a kit – and because they are not seen as a priority.

And yet, despite all these statistics and the huge injustice, one common response that I hear over and over again is that the #MeToo movement is bound to result in false allegations and damage to the careers of innocent men.

Given our paltry justice system, perhaps it is no surprise that Twitter has become a modern-day confessional. In early 2014, the #YesAllWomen hashtag began to trend in response to the Isla Vista killings by incel Elliot Rodger. Rodger left behind a 140-page manifesto that dripped with bile and misogyny, declaring,

> 'My hatred and rage towards all women festered inside me like a plague. Their very existence is the cause of all of my torture, pain and suffering throughout my life… Why do women behave like vicious, stupid, cruel animals who take delight in my suffering and starvation?… I concluded that women are flawed. There is something mentally wrong with the way their brains are wired, as if they haven't evolved from animal-like thinking. They are incapable of reason or thinking rationally. They are like animals, completely controlled by their primal, depraved emotions and impulses.'

In response came the #NotAllMen hashtag. Many sought to assert that Rodger's views were not typical of the male sex, and I do respect this caveat. But millions of women pointed out that his behaviour – though indeed a result of breakdown and severe mental illness – had been fed by an internet culture of incel misogyny, and, though it represented an extremity of American culture, it was on a spectrum with other shades of male behaviour. They shared stories of assault, misogyny, harassment, male aggression, hostility. Tweets ranged from '#YesAllWomen because every time I try to say that I want gender equality I have to explain that I don't hate men' to 'When women trust men, we're naïve idiots who should've known better. When women fear men, we're hysterical, paranoid feminazis' (Kendall Mckenzie).

When Alyssa Milano (eleven years after Tarana Burke first conceptualized the term) tweeted 'if you've been sexually assaulted or harassed, write metoo as a reply to this tweet', she went to bed with no idea that it was going to snowball. Over a two-week period, there were 1.7 million tweets; 12 million Facebook posts. On Twitter, the topic trended in eighty-five countries. In an intensification of the imagery of feminism as 'waves', it was couched in the metaphor of natural disaster: a flood, a tsunami, an avalanche. It was significant because the world finally woke up and listened. Many had no intention of attempting to try their accusers online, without due process. They just wanted to be heard. They wanted to share pain that had been locked inside for months, years.

In the aftermath of the #MeToo movement came the infamous Shitty Media Men list. This was a private spreadsheet, created by Moira Donegan, to highlight men in the New York media and publishing sphere who had been abusive to women, ranging across a spectrum of bad behaviour from 'weird lunches' and creepy come-ons to serious assault. It was posted in October 2017. The document was prefaced by the disclaimer, 'This document is only a collection of misconduct allegations and rumours. Take everything with a grain of salt.'

Initially it was shared with eight other women. It was developed as a tool to help and empower women – a whisper network of warnings. Donegan herself has noted that it was never intended to be 'a weapon'. Its function was more akin to a protective shield. But soon the list got out of her control. In an echo of #MeToo, she was taken aback at the number of people who posted about their bad experiences, at the outpouring of pain as women recounted being beaten, drugged and raped, making her realize that 'many of us had weathered more than we had been willing to admit to one another'. Even though she quickly took the list down, it had been shared and photographed; an article appeared on BuzzFeed; someone posted it on Reddit. Donegan lost her job and found herself iced out by various media people who saw her as tainted, or because of uneasy loyalty to their male friends on the list.

Whisper lists and Twitter trials are not the best way forward, but they have been necessary due to a broken justice system. Those who argue for due process, for the importance of 'innocence until proven guilty', have a fair point. So let us hope that #MeToo enables victims to feel that they can come forward and be listened to, that rape is taken seriously as a crime, in order to fortify the justice system and enable it to do its job properly.

# IX

Kit Gruelle, who features in the HBO documentary *Private Violence*, made the following observation about abusive men: 'Abusers have enormous egos, an enormous need to be the centre of attention. They have a sense of entitlement. They expect everything is going to go their way all the time, and when it doesn't, they reach for their toolbox.'

I was reminded of this when I interviewed another survivor of an abusive relationship, who told me about her experiences of dating a narcissistic chauvo-feminist:

K was charming, charismatic and extremely good-looking: a cross between Elvis and Justin Bieber. I met him when I was in my early twenties. I was living in Australia, in a commune in an abandoned cookie factory. I was also in a vulnerable place. My stepfather had recently given me a settlement of around $150,000 as compensation for the childhood abuse he'd inflicted on me, though his contract had specified this covered the abuse he had done 'in the past' and that which he might do 'in the future'.

Having escaped him, I was staying between the commune and at my biological father's house, but our relationship was in a shaky, strange place. My ability to have a relationship with him, and other memories of my family, had been destroyed by the abuse. I felt distant from them, isolated in the world.

K and I met at a house party where he was the DJ. He and I spoke, and I learned he had been DJing that summer at festivals in Europe and then in clubs in the winter. We ended up spending the night together. He seemed enamoured of me. He behaved as though I was a goddess. He told me that he had a dream of operating his own label and had immigrated here to make it happen.

It wasn't long before we moved in together. We chose a house overlooking a remote forest. My compensation cheque covered the costs; I was paying for our bills, our food, his DJ equipment. His belief in his gifts wasn't delusional. A record label did offer him a huge contract, but he turned it down, arguing that it would be tainted by corporate greed. But his idealism regarding his music bordered on narcissism, for he believed that he was a shaman and that his music could heal people. If this sounds absurd, then you should know that on the rave scene the DJ does become a messiah figure when they're performing a set. They play to a room full of people who have taken drugs, surrendered their minds and reason to acid, ecstasy, cocaine, ketamine. The DJ dictates the music, and thus the mood; he literally controls their hive mind, spinning it this way and that. That power is hugely attractive to women, so the DJ is perennially surrounded by the temptation of adoring groupies. K revelled in all this. I used to joke that he would have made a good cult leader.

K also believed that he had healing energies which he released when he had sex with a woman. His typical chat-up line would be to offer them a massage. This might sound creepy, but he always couched this in feminist principles. He behaved as though he was a champion of women. He bowed down to them; he worshipped them; he spoke about the divine feminine. He said that women were stronger than men and that women should be in charge. He believed, however, that he was literally God's gift to women.

The honeymoon phase in our relationship lasted a few weeks. And then, one day, a woman turned up on our doorstep. The moment she came into the house, her sexual energy was immediately apparent, and I asked what was going on. K said that he wanted to have a threesome.

I didn't want to sleep with her, and I didn't want her to sleep with him. But they kept trying to cajole me into it. In a state of shock, I went out onto the deck and tried to escape the situation by meditating. I was actually having a blissful experience, one of the most intense experiences of my life, in fact. With my eyes closed, I had the sensation that I no longer had a body and was just consciousness shooting through deep space, the most calm and peaceful I have ever known before or since.

Suddenly, K tapped me on the shoulder and yanked me back into the house. I was disorientated and suffering from dissociation; I felt strangely light, like a balloon on a string. The woman was now naked, and they kept encouraging me to join in. I refused. Eventually, they went into a bedroom and left the door ajar. I sat in the living room and watched them fucking.

I started crying and ran out of the house. In the depths of the forest, I felt utter despair and did not want to be alive any more; I prayed for the angels to take me away. After some hours, I returned to the house. The woman was gone, and K was anxious. He said, 'I've been so worried about you. Where did you go?'

That's when he made his big confession: that he was unable to adhere to monogamy. He needed to share himself with many women. He justified this as a spiritual path, for he believed in tantra, and sex, for him, was a way to enlightenment.

You might wonder why I didn't walk away at this point, but I was lost in a fog: young, naïve, vulnerable, very much in love with him, and keen to be a good person, to dissolve my ego. I told myself that this was a test from the universe and that I had to learn to accept the situation. I told myself: if I love him, then I must accept him for who he is. He always reassured me that he loved me above all the others, that I was his number one.

This went on for four years. We left the US for Mexico, by which time we'd run through all the money I had. We hitchhiked to Brazil. I felt ground down by our poverty; we were homeless, living on the streets, hitching rides to go anywhere there was a party. Eventually we made it to Europe, where we lived in Italy with some promoters that he knew. As a non-EU citizen I couldn't work, so I had no ability to earn and liberate myself from our poverty. By then, I had lost touch with my family and I felt trapped by our relationship. I was in a state of shock that we had fallen so low and had no idea what to do. I felt guilty and ashamed that we constantly relied on others to take care of us.

K was sleeping with numerous other women. Often, he would gaslight me. He would tell me that he was going out to meet a promoter and I would find out that he was going to meet another woman. Sometimes he would deny his affairs; sometimes he'd admit to them. I felt disorientated. His mix of lies and honesty left me with a warped sense of what was going on, destabilized me. He would try to placate me by reassuring me that they didn't mean as much to him as I did. He would tell me that I was the one he was meant to be with.

Next, we travelled to Ibiza. On one occasion, because I was unable to find the way to a rave, he hit me. On another, he abandoned me entirely to go chasing after a girl. I was left by the side of the road with no money. I ended up sleeping in a cave on the beach. I was taken in by a twenty-year-old Italian man, who was kind to me, took care of me and didn't force himself on me. Finally, he lent me $100, and I was able to get a boat off the island and hitchhiked my way to Germany, where I ended up staying in a squat in Berlin.

K followed me there. Our romance started up again, but this time, fed up, I had a one-night stand with someone else. When I told K, he went absolutely crazy. He yelled at me. He yelled at everyone. He grabbed a fire extinguisher and sprayed it about. Finally, our relationship ended.

Ten years later, I got an email from him. He addressed the one-night stand I'd had and wrote, 'I am finally able to forgive you.' Then he asked me to marry him.

I said no.

# X

Eventually, the confrontation came: I stood up to R in private, clumsily, but a point was made. After that, things only got worse. It felt like a declaration of war. He retaliated in various, mostly petty ways. A few friends went quiet on me; a few berated me. They are not really to blame. On one occasion, I pulled out of accompanying a friend to an event I realized R would be at with a lame, last-minute excuse that understandably annoyed her. I wanted to keep my battle with him private, and I was therefore quite vague, evasive about why we had fallen out.

Just as uncertainty began to vex me – *Had I been too harsh? Had I made a mistake?* – I encountered another woman who'd had a bad experience with R. She was very young and keen to get her first job in academia. He had wanted to sleep with her; she hadn't, and he'd turned on her, got nasty. Again, the tainted relief rushed through me: *It's not just me…*

I thought about reaching out to her. But what if R found out that I was making contact with her? I'd heard from a mutual female friend that R was anxious about being outed, due to the rising tide of #MeToo confessions. I dreaded that he might make a pre-emptive strike against me through smears or the whisper network. In those final weeks and months before he was finally brought down, Weinstein resorted to extreme measures, hiring Mossad agents to follow journalists who were working on exposing him. It was as though a desperation made him take increasingly reckless gambles, so close was he to public moral bankruptcy.

In more optimistic moments, I wondered if all those feminist articles that R was tweeting might seep into his consciousness. The social change frothing around him might invoke a shift in his individual psyche, a reframing of his behaviour from 'laddish fun' to 'abuse of women'. Was he capable of change, I wondered, and, given that there was a global conversation taking place, would he re-examine himself?

Thomas Page McBee changed his sex at the age of thirty. In a video interview for the Aspen Festival of Ideas (2018), he related how this gave him insight into the way society shapes male behaviour. He noticed immediately that 'I gained a lot of privileges, I lost a lot of connection' and was frequently criticized for being 'too vulnerable'. His verdict on Weinstein is that 'you're not seeing an extreme form of an innate state' but 'you're seeing an extreme form of socialized behaviour'. He cited a longitudinal study conducted by Niobe Way, a developmental psychologist at New York University, who studied adolescent boys and male friendships for decades. She found a pattern: at the age of sixteen, boys start to disconnect from their friends. They are socialized out of 'being empathetic, sensitive, expressing affection or being vulnerable' for fear of being 'girly' or 'gay'.

When it comes to male and female behaviour, there is an ongoing debate which revolves around biology versus socialization. Is it genetically determined for men to be more aggressive and women to be more passive, men to prey on and women to beguile, men to be promiscuous and women to be monogamous, and so on? There's a tired, clichéd argument that runs along the lines of 'once upon a time, men were hunter-gatherers and went out to roam and find food and women stayed at home, and that's why we're hardwired to behave the way we do now'. I have seen many blogs and commentators online justifying bad male behaviour, harassment and assault on this basis. They argue that it will take a long time for us to adapt to the #MeToo movement because we need to undo thousands of years of biological tendencies.

Using science to justify sexism has been going on for over a century. Once upon a time, Darwin made the argument in *On the Origin of Species*. Men, he declared, have the 'unfortunate birthright' of competitiveness which resulted from having to compete for women. Their higher achievements in the workplace are not due to social causes but biology: constant fighting and hunting has led to greater 'observation, reason, invention or imagination'. In our current society, we can see that equal educational opportunities have proved him wrong. In 2019, in the UK, 25.3 per cent of girls got top grades of A (or 7) at GCSE, compared to 18.6 per cent of boys in Year 11, at age sixteen.

Some thinkers have built on Darwinian theory to argue that sexual aggression is an evolved adaptation in human males. In her groundbreaking work *Against Our Will*, Susan Brownmiller overturned this idea by declaring that rape was motivated by a desire for power and domination rather than sexual arousal. But, in 2000, evolutionary biologists Randy Thornhill and Craig T. Palmer published *A Natural History of Rape: Biological Bases of Sexual Coercion*, in which they argued that rape evolved as an 'alternative dating strategy' and that 'We fervently believe that, just as the leopard's spots and the giraffe's elongated neck are the result of aeons of past Darwinian selection, so is rape.' (Presumably the image of the leopard also implies that such spots can't be changed.) Therefore, they argued, contemporary rape-prevention policies were doomed to fail. But numerous scientists have pointed out the flaws in this.

After all, if rape has evolutionary advantages, then why do men rape children, or other men – such tendencies would surely have been eliminated in the course of evolution as they didn't confer reproductive advantage on our ancestors. Furthermore, studies have shown that rapists are not commonly motivated by sexual deprivation; they tend to have *more* consensual partners than other men; and married rapists are just as likely to have active sex lives with their wives.

The subtext of these sexist science arguments is often that women can't expect any better from men, so we've just got to put up with bad behaviour, or – as Thornhill and Palmer argue – that because it is innate, women are the ones who have to adapt by dressing more modestly. Equally, it is offensive to men, suggesting they are animalistic beasts who cannot control their hardwired lustful instincts. Cordelia Fine defines this fallacy as the pseudoscience of neurosexism. Our gender wiring is soft, not hard – 'it is flexible, malleable and changeable'. Scientist Lise Eliot also explains that 'All such skills are learned and neuro-plasticity – the modifications of neurons and their connections in response to experience – trumps hard-wiring every time.'

Therefore, what science does tell us is that we do not have to shrug our shoulders and put up with a society in which assault or abuse is inevitable. Biology is malleable, and culture is ever-changing. Once upon a time, we believed in hanging criminals, in beating children for their mistakes. From century to century, decade to decade, year to year, we evolve; our values change and so does our behaviour.

This is why I am wary of the term 'toxic masculinity' and am cautious in using it. Feminists rightly argue that its original meaning did not refer to masculinity per se but an extreme form of gendered behaviour. However, as it has entered the mainstream, its meaning has evolved and expanded into a blurry generalization about the male sex. It is a mirror of the Eve myth, whereby women were once seen as inherently tainted because of the first female's fall in the Garden of Eden. It can be taken to imply that there is something biologically evil in men, and I do not agree that this is the case. I feel that the term 'patriarchy' is far more useful, a social and cultural force that has shaped us over centuries – and thus created conditions in which rape is more culturally acceptable. In 1990, sociologist Diana Scully conducted a study, 'Understanding Sexual Violence', for the US National Institute of Mental Health. She found that many rapists who end up in jail assumed they'd never be punished, seeing rape as 'a rewarding, low-risk act'. They tended to lack empathy for women, but they also believed it would be excused by their peers. She concluded that most rapes are therefore not driven by psychopathology but sociocultural values; they are the result of 'rape culture', which is why there are large variations in the numbers of self-confessed rapists from one country to another. In a 2013 *Lancet* study, 22.7 per cent of men in China admitted to rape (either partner or non-partner) compared to 31.9 per cent in Indonesia and 60.7 per cent in Papua New Guinea. The anthropologist Peggy Reeves Sanday has also extensively studied the socio-cultural context of rape and found that it tends to be more common in societies with ideologies of toughness and a lack of female participation in politics.

Once the Weinstein revelations burst, *How did he get away with it for so long?* was the question that everyone asked.

His behaviour was aided by a social structure that allowed him to carry on acting as he did. Rose McGowan has referred to Hollywood as 'an organized system for abusing women… it's an entire machine, a supply chain', and 'if white men could have a playground, this would be it'.

Those individuals who did enable him, who maintained the status quo, were not simply conspirators who were turning a blind eye because they wanted to maintain profit (though that was a factor, at times). In the *Untouchable* documentary, some of the bad attitudes posited come from men who look and sound dazed, confused and naive about women and have a rather low opinion of the role they should play in the world. One gossip columnist confessed that 'I always imagined that actresses wanted to sleep with Harvey because it was good for their career... for any powerful man in any city, women are part of the thing'. The word 'thing', one presumes, is a synonym for 'harem', the pool of women you can automatically sleep with once you get into your position of power.

Another woman interviewed pointed out that when an actress was hired to work on Miramax films, there was an underlying assumption that she'd got the part because 'she'd slept with Harvey', never that 'he'd slept with her'. Women were seen as actively seeking out his bed, merrily prostituting themselves on the casting couch in order to get their roles, and this was all fine and normal. Weinstein himself made use of that social atmosphere. Erika Rosenbaum was told by him, 'Everybody does this', as though it was just part of the Hollywood experience, and he would then rattle off the names of a number of younger actresses who had boosted their careers by sleeping with him.

This dire attitude is one that has gone on for many decades. Women have bought into it, too. You only have to look at how people responded to Naomi Wolf back in 2004. She came out and reported the sexual harassment she had experienced at the hands of Harold Bloom when she was a student at Yale twenty years earlier. The *Guardian* gathered a series of statements from women in response to the question 'Was Wolf right to speak out?' There were a few supportive replies, for example from Andrea Dworkin, who responded: 'We are not friends. I dislike everything she has ever written. But she would not lie or exaggerate, especially not about a matter of sexual harassment. She has done her time in a rape counselling service – she knows what women go through when they come out with allegations of sexual harassment, the backlash they experience.' But for the most part, I am sure many of the women now look back on the things they said and cringe. Here's a selection of a few:

JENNI MURRAY: As far as Wolf is concerned, it's a little bit late, frankly. And I would have thought that someone with such a mouth on her would have said something at the time. I've always thought she was a sensible, solid young woman, who wrote well… I certainly don't believe that because she's pretty she should not have an opinion. But young women need strong role models who don't portray themselves as victims.

MARCELLE D'ARGY SMITH: I think she has done us no favours. I think she sounds ludicrous. I thought she was going to say he put his tongue down her throat or something. Man puts hand on thigh: well, wow! I think to make these allegations now is cruel, self-serving and unnecessary. If she was outraged at the time, it's not as if she was a woman without ammunition. It's not like trying to claim compensation from the Nazis. I'm sure tons of lecturers have put hands on thighs.

CAMILLE PAGLIA: I just feel it's indecent that if Naomi Wolf did not have the courage to pursue the matter at the time, then to bring all of this down on a man who is in his seventies and has health problems, to drag him into a 'he said, she said' scenario so late in the game, to me demonstrates a lack of proportion and a basic sense of fair play. It really smacks of the Salem witch-hunts and all the accompanying hysteria. It really grates on me that Naomi Wolf for her entire life has been batting her eyes and bobbing her boobs in the face of men and made a profession out of courting male attention.

When you compare this – from just fifteen years ago – to the present day, you can see how fundamentally our ideas about consent, about the respect that women deserve, have advanced.

# X I

Later that summer, I heard an anecdote about R's attitudes to women. One that I wished I'd heard before I'd slept with him rather than after. When I asked a colleague of R's if he thought R was a misogynist, his immediate response was, 'Yes. I've sat with him in a group of men and heard him say, "So what are your strategies for seducing women? Tell me your techniques."' A group discussion had unfolded where they had shared tips on how to get women into bed, mostly the sort that you might read in *The Game* and suchlike.

In that respect, R is no different from many men who have been socialized to view women in this way. CBS News grouped together a number of successful men (including film-maker Judd Apatow, astronaut Leland D. Melvin and chef Tom Colicchio) to discuss the issue. Mark Herzlich, an American footballer, remarked that bad attitudes to women are nurtured during adolescence: 'Men are grouped together from a young age – whether it's athletic teams or the locker rooms or fraternities – and in a collective group of men there becomes a vernacular that is negative towards women and there becomes an expectation on other men to play on an ideology of conquering women.'

Men's rights activists (MRAs) argue that life is not easy for men. Warren Farrell, author of *The Myth of Male Power*, points out that while women can be reduced to 'sex objects', men can be caricatured as 'success objects'. However, I think that much of MRA aggression reflects a pain which also stems from a desire to be free from gender stereotypes as well, from the way that misogyny undermines and cages men as well as women.

In an interview for the *Independent*, Jack Urwin, author of *Man Up: Surviving Modern Masculinity*, explained that 'The fact is, a lot of men seem to feel their place in the modern world is becoming less purposeful… So in an attempt to claw back some sense of manliness a lot of them are perpetuating… a sort of overcompensating form of behaviour that has its roots in ideas of traditional masculinity – such as strength and stoicism. But because our understanding of these has become so warped and removed from context they end up just being very unhealthy ways to act.'

Men are far more likely to die from suicide than women. In the US, Canada and Britain, the worst-hit group are middle-aged men, who often suffer in greater numbers than any other age group from unemployment and divorce. Relationship breakdowns are more likely to drive a man to suicide because he is more isolated, whereas women may have a support network of friendships.

In the UK, 2.5 million men report having no close friends. Men tend to have fewer friends as they age; Professor Damien Ridge observes that 'Loneliness in older men is a real issue, and many men in their 30s already show signs of heading that way. Compared with women, the men who see me for psychotherapy are emotionally isolated. I'm sometimes the only person they've opened up to.' Indeed, the way that society has socialized men into repressing emotions and vulnerabilities has caused pain for centuries. In the aftermath of the First World War, men who returned with shell shock were seen as 'cowardly', threatened with court martial, their trauma downplayed and denied, for society was in love with the idea of male heroes returning from the front full of courage and bravery.

While men are penalized for expressing their emotions, they are rewarded in the workplace for aggressive behaviour. A 2015 study shows that if male leaders ask for help or display modesty they are viewed as less competent and capable. Female bosses who show empathy are rewarded, but agreeable men who show warmth and sympathy earn an average of 18 per cent less. Basically, men are penalized for behaving as decent human beings in the workplace. One of the main themes that you see in confessions from men who have fallen in the #MeToo era is the cold shock of waking up and seeing the impact of their actions. Lorin Stein, who stepped down from the *Paris Review* after allegations hit him, reflected that 'The way I behaved was hurtful, degrading and infuriating to a degree that I have only begun to understand in the past month.' Men have not been encouraged to develop imaginative empathy, self-awareness, sensitivity; now, should they fail to, it could prove fatal for their careers. We need to give them the space to develop these attributes, praise for developing them, allow them to flourish.

During his decades of inflicting abuse, Weinstein was often encouraged to have therapy. In fact, when Zelda Perkins received a settlement from him, she stipulated in the contract that he must go to therapy for a minimum of a year and that she would attend the first session with him. But she had no idea if he ever attended the sessions, and she found the stipulation impossible to enforce.

According to Germaine Greer, the #MeToo movement has infantilized women, an accusation which has been echoed elsewhere. But if you apply this to Weinstein and the women he targeted, it doesn't hold up. He was physically much stronger than them, propped up by a power structure which allowed him to play the 'sheriff in town', enabled by colleagues, and was given the time and space to spend years honing and refining his bullying techniques. Weinstein was the infant, not the women. He behaved like a boy who could not understand that women were not objects to play with like toys. When they did not comply, he threw temper tantrums. When people tried to get him to have therapy, he failed to listen. This would have presented him with an opportunity to reflect on his actions like a grown-up. It might have saved numerous women from his abuse; it might have saved his career. But, instead, he remained in stasis. When he was finally accused by over a hundred women, he declared that all the sex he'd had was consensual. Hope D'Amore said that she thought Weinstein probably genuinely believed this because his attitude was that he deserved to have whatever he wanted, and if he achieved fulfilment that meant 'yes'.

This lack of empathy is simplistically childlike. Being a citizen of society involves a compromise, a stand-off between individual desire and civilized norms. We cannot rampage through life doing whatever we please. We do not steal our neighbour's beautiful car, no matter how much we covet it, because society is governed by a pact of trust, and if we fail to maintain that pact we are punished. One of my male friends once remarked to me that women invite rape if they wear revealing clothes. In response, I pointed out that, following his logic, if he headed out into town one night driving a hot red sports car, a nice suit and an expensive watch, a mugger would have every right to steal from him and beat him up because he was putting his wealth on display. The process of growing up involves learning laws and moral codes and developing empathy and respect for others. When it comes to harassment and treatment of women, that tension has been too slack, with selfish, individual desire taking precedence. Now, with #MeToo, the lines have been drawn more clearly. We have redefined what it is to be civilized.

# XII

Social change occurs slowly. It progresses through push and pull, a tug of war between those who want to move forward and those who want to maintain the status quo.

Often the backlash takes two forms. First, such progress is deemed 'irrational', compared to a previous norm of reason and common sense. 'The world has gone mad!' is the response, the subtext being that 'women have gone mad'. It is a macro-argument of the way abused women are discredited, such as Ronan Farrow being assured that Rose McGowan's complaints about Weinstein had no substance because 'She's crazy!'

Writing in *The Spectator*, Douglas Murray explored some examples of men who have fallen in the aftermath of #MeToo, including one left-wing journalist – 'his career too was dashed to the floor by people high on the octane of unreflective moral outrage'. In *The Madness of Crowds: Gender, Race and Identity*, he asserts that women's rights gained traction and fulfilment in the twentieth century and 'appeared to be reaching some sort of settlement'. But then 'just as the train appeared to be reaching its desired destination it suddenly picked up steam and went crashing off down the tracks and into the distance'. However, this represents an argument that veers close to gaslighting on a more generalized level. The implication is that, in this utopia of equality that we're supposedly in, any experience of misogyny is the product of feverish female imagination, a wilful and determined desire to seek out prejudice. Murray is right that we should celebrate the gains that have been made, but history demonstrates that such gains can be fragile, that we can move forward and then back. I'm sure that if you asked the average American woman living under the Obama presidency whether she thought the right to abortion would be rescinded, she'd reply confidently in the negative. Yet, in the land of the free, the female right to terminate a pregnancy is reversing, with eleven states restricting abortion rights in 2019.

Murray does make some useful points about the need for love and tolerance, and the dangers of reacting to #MeToo in the vengeful spirit of 'over-correction'. But if such tolerance is gained by having to blinker yourself to uncomfortable new stories and whitewash tragedies, then I feel this may only create more division, and greater polarization in the long run. Love and tolerance also require patience, empathy and an ability to listen.

The second form is that of nostalgia. As Grayson Perry sums up so beautifully:

Feminism has always been forward-looking. Women's rights will come, a woman's role will change and expand, she is working for a better, a more just future. Women seem to embrace change, not just in society, but in themselves. In order to take up this expanding role she needs to adapt, learn new skills, become more confident. Men though, always seem to be harking back to some mythical golden age (for men) when men were 'men'. A time of hunting (dangerous, thrilling), a time of war (dangerous, thrilling and boring), a time of heavy industry (dangerous, boring), times when all the vintage men equipment – anger, violence, physical strength – could be put through its paces. A time also when men dominated women.

Many of the reactions to the #MeToo movement echo earlier moments in history when seismic change has occurred. When the suffragettes fought for women to have the right to vote, they were opposed by both male and female organizations. Lord Curzon, head of the National League for Opposing Woman Suffrage, argued that 'political activity will tend to take woman away from her proper sphere and highest duty, which is maternity'. Curzon also felt that 'women have not, as a sex, or a class, the calmness of temperament, or the balance of mind... necessary to qualify them to exercise a weighty judgement in political affairs'. In the Women's National Anti-Suffrage League, Mary Ward minimized the debate by declaring that it was really just 'a sex rivalry, which has too often masqueraded as reform'. However, as Julia Bush has noted: 'In many ways the suffrage and anti-suffrage movements were interdependent, reacting to each other's arguments, responding to each other's tactics, and connecting as well as clashing across the wider arenas of male politics and female social action.'

We can see a similar pattern occurring today, with a push and a pull between those who belittle #MeToo as a witch-hunt and those who want to see it bring about change. According to Meghan Daum, women can also be guilty of a gap between private and public self, between feminist-woke persona and inner conviction. In a recent article for the *Guardian*, where she positioned herself as an 'older feminist', she asks the question, 'Am I allowed nuanced feelings about #MeToo?' She goes on to say, 'In the *New York Times*, Daphne Merkin identified a gulf between what women said publicly about #MeToo and the eye-rolling that went on in private. "Publicly, they say the right things, expressing approval and joining in the chorus of voices that applaud the takedown of maleficent characters who prey on vulnerable women in the workplace," she wrote. "In private it's a different story. 'Grow up, this is real life,' I hear these same feminist friends say".'

This is not something I've yet come across in any women I know. Time and time again, when I interviewed women, I found that they were relieved, pleased, empowered by #MeToo. Nobody was rolling their eyes. They acknowledged that there were still complexities left to be discussed; they also felt concerned that men should not be villainized and should be part of the conversation. But, for them, the #MeToo movement was one that they championed with sincerity.

Daum has also argued in a piece for *Medium* that we should not criticize men but instead address our own issues with toxic femininity. I agree that women are not angels, nor perfect, nor do we always tell the truth, but I don't think anyone arguing for #MeToo is suggesting we deify women, only that we pay attention to the stories being shared, listen hard, and consider how to improve a society that has enabled abuse to take place. Within her article, there is no acknowledgement of the fact that the world is not a level playing field between men and women. If, at the same time that Weinstein had been brought down, there had been a female boss who had abused around a hundred men and forced them to have sex with her, this might have given her story weight. Nor do we have Hillary Clinton bragging about jerking off on some younger guy and 'grabbing him by the dick'. Daum does acknowledge that #MeToo is important but declares that the #BelieveWomen hashtag is 'hollow sloganeering' for 'its suggestion that women are some monolithic entity that is inherently more moral, innocent, or trustworthy than men, is not just reductive but insulting'. But the fact is that her world view does not need to be argued. Most of the time, the world doesn't believe women. The rape conviction stats prove that.

Often when people are trying to undermine #MeToo, they focus on the trivial. They will cite the ambiguous Aziz Ansari/Grace story but ignore the more serious cases. They will zone in on one absurd example and conflate it, or focus on one detail which grates. Meghan Daum's reaction to the Shitty Media Men list, for example, is one of concern about women complaining about 'a weird lunch' date and 'lumping' this in with serious crimes such as rape: '"Weird lunch!" I said to more than one person. "Welcome to publishing! I'm going to write a memoir about my early days in New York and call it *Weird Lunch*".'

But I know that one of the men on that list has done considerable harm to women – has psychologically scarred them for years – and so to overly focus on a weird lunch is to miss the real damage some of those men inflicted. Furthermore, the list's creator, Moira Donegan, has herself pointed out that they are not equating a weird lunch and rape as crimes of the same severity – merely that they are on a wide spectrum. The list was not a court judgment but a warning, implying that a man's creepy behaviour might signal the start of worse to come.

That Daum titles her *Guardian* article 'nuanced' is telling. It is a word that is increasingly used to undermine the #MeToo movement, to suggest that the response is hysterical. There is often an underlying sexism to the term, implying that women cannot cope with the complexity of working out the difference between, say, flirting and assault, that they lack the rationale and reason. But a recent survey for *Vox* proved the opposite. Interestingly, it showed that those who were most concerned about #MeToo were also those who supported it with the most conviction. They were aware of its danger and the possibility of over-correction; they wanted to see nuanced and fair responses and punishments.

I am glad that Daum was honest enough to express her views, which are risky and controversial in the current climate. But, ultimately, I find them disappointing, just as I did Germaine Greer saying that #MeToo is a 'whingeing' movement and that we should ditch rape as a crime because 'Rape is a daily crime, it's not spectacular. What we need is a coherent law of sexual assault.' Daum herself has concluded that the conversation about #MeToo has begun 'to split down generational lines'. Perhaps it is also a matter of social norms that are hard to shake off once you have grown up with them. Daum says that she was taught 'If the drunk guy sitting next to you at the wedding reception gets fresh, kick him in the shins', which implies an era when women were the ones responsible for handling assault and rape; it was up to them to fight it rather than men having to take any sort of personal responsibility. Women should be empowered, as I have argued earlier in my essay, but we cannot do all the work. While such mores might have 'toughened women up', it clearly didn't solve the problem, or else the Weinstein scandal and #MeToo era would never have happened. Indeed, as female rights have improved over the past few decades, women have developed higher expectations (as I did) of equality, which, in effect, has made the problem more glaring, given that male behaviour might not have changed in line with them.

Jordan Peterson has declared that he is not anti-feminist and not averse to women entering the workplace. But he has also criticized radical feminists and fears that masculinity is currently under 'attack'. I am not implying that Peterson is a chauvo-feminist by any means, only citing this range of his viewpoints in the interests of balance; his followers often complain that Peterson's ideas have been misrepresented, their nuance lacking, though it is not always easy to pin them down.

Peterson has expressed a nostalgia for life in the 1950s. He is critical of Betty Friedan's iconic feminist text *The Feminine Mystique* (1963), where Friedan captured the voice of a generation of women when she wrote: 'We can no longer ignore that voice within women that says, "I want something more than my husband and my children and my home".' Peterson's response to it is: 'it's so whiny; it's just enough to drive a modern person mad to listen to those suburban housewives from the late 50s ensconced in their secure, comfortable lives complaining about the fact that they're bored because they don't have enough opportunity'. He suggests that they ought to have just got a hobby. Interviewed for his views on the #MeToo movement, he mused that 'we are going to soon remember why sex was traditionally enshrined in marriage', though we should not forget that Weinstein was a married man, and, for the women he abused, he became a force of chaos in their lives – a chaos they needed an antidote from. Peterson also mulled on the impact of women being able to control their reproductive freedom: 'What does that make women? Because now, they're a new biological entity. And so, it's wide open. What are women now? We don't know.'

Sometimes it can be easier to view the past with nostalgia. It becomes a utopian comfort blanket, a time when Things Were Better and Simpler. Shifts in laws, culture, behaviour can be messy and complex. But they are also part of growth.

Peterson's views (and, likewise, Daum's) do not particularly shock or surprise me because I am friends with older men who have similar viewpoints. They are different from my younger male friends, who are far more likely to see me as a multifaceted character.

One of my older male friends has a tendency to see women as archetypes: mothers, vessels for reproduction, creatures of body rather than mind. Another, who was two decades older than me, would often thwart the depth of connection between us by his narrow ideas of the female sex. He saw women in Mars/Venus terms, as emotional, romantic, less rational, thirsty for marriage/commitment. We'd be hanging out, enjoying a film, laughing over a joke together, discussing current affairs, when he'd suddenly come out with words that jolted me. Words that made me roll my eyes and sigh and think, *What the hell?* such as, 'It's just so amazing that you're able to read a map!' as I successfully gave him navigational instructions during a road trip, a task I did not find complex or taxing, nor one which I had to strain against my vagina to accomplish.

It is tough to experience casual chauvinism or misogyny from people you know and like – to see it spring not from hatred but a kind of pastel ignorance, ideas that have seeped into the psyche from society since birth. They have grown up with it; one friend confessed that he saw his father openly referring to his mother as 'the weaker sex'. I also feel a little sorry for my older male friends because they are keen to have loving relationships, but their views hinder them from connecting with women and being able to find a girlfriend.

In a recent *GQ* survey where over 1,000 men were interviewed about their reactions to the #MeToo movement, one thread that cropped up in their reporting was that 'younger men acknowledge the problem, but older men tend to dismiss it as overblown'.

In another survey, conducted by YouGov, it was found that more than a third of over-65s do not regard non-consensual sex in marriage or a relationship as rape, compared with 16 per cent of people aged 16 to 24. And 42 per cent of over-65s said that if sexual activity continues after a woman changes her mind, it is not rape, compared with 22 per cent of the 25s–49s.

The skewed ideas of consent that exist today are rooted in social attitudes of the past. We can trace back their tendrils over the course of centuries. In Ancient Greece, it was regarded as a greater sin for a man to have consensual sex with another man's wife than it was for him to rape her. Rapists got a doubled fine, while adulterous seducers suffered the death penalty. Women tended to be split into two stereotypes: good girls and bad girls, the virgin and the whore, simplified to angelic, sexless exaltation or denigrated to a gutter sex temptress selling her body. This has resulted in a scenario where men would have a wife as his 'angel in the home' and recourse to a brothel to sate his sexual hunger – a practice that still exists in some contemporary societies.

*Les Liaisons Dangereuses* captures the dilemma this created for women, who had to conceal their desires and adopt a mask of chastity so that they slotted into the 'good girl' category. Let us return to the scene

I mentioned earlier, involving the deflowering of the virginal Cécile de Volanges by the rake the Vicomte de Valmont. It is a scene that hovers in a grey area between consent and rape. Soon after, Cécile writes to her mentor, the Marquise de Merteuil, for advice. She is told that she should embrace Valmont's tutelage and her new-found sexuality. Effectively, Merteuil gives her permission to be a sexual creature and to take pleasure in seduction, declaring that the 'shame that love brings with it is no different from the pain: it is only felt once… The pleasure, however, remains…' Merteuil regularly mocks Valmont. She pricks his grandiose ego by suggesting that he has foolish ideas about the women he has supposedly 'conquered'. She points out:

> Tell me then, languishing lover: the women you have had – do you imagine you violated them? Don't you know that however willing, however eager we are to give ourselves, we must nonetheless have an excuse? And is there any more convenient than an appearance of yielding to force? […] which keeps up an appearance of taking by storm even what we are quite prepared to surrender.

What is the subtext of this? That women mean yes when they say no. Unfortunately, this is a social norm that women once had to collude in. Women were forced to feign an appearance of resisting sexual advances – even when welcome – because they were expected to act the part of the virginal woman. Female sexuality was shameful and had to be veiled by an illusion of innocence. As Merteuil says in an earlier letter, one wrong word and a woman's reputation could be ruined, her marriage prospects over. Women who feigned chastity also played to male desires to turn courtship into a game where they were the active predators. As Merteuil points out, women effectively humour Valmont so that he can take pleasure in thinking he has 'conquered' them.

Society has become more accepting of female sexuality, the shame gradually seeping away, so that one of our recent national treasures is Fleabag, the complex, sexually voracious heroine of Phoebe Waller-Bridge's hugely successful comedy (although I am amused by Waller-Bridge's observation that women say they feel an affinity for her heroine while men tend to regard her as filthy).

However, the idea of yes meaning no has existed for longer than no meaning no, and still permeates our society. These days, it is often echoed in the internet porn that teenage boys watch, thus educating them back into the mistakes of the past.

Before you worry that I am being horrifically ageist, then know that I am only a few years younger than Meghan Daum and was born on the cusp of Generations X and Y. I know many men and women older than me who have discussed these topics with me with such wisdom, balance and insight; I admire thinkers such as bell hooks, Baroness Helena Kennedy, Susan Brownmiller, Rebecca Solnit and Tony Porter. What I am criticizing is not the older generation but 'older' ideas and an unwillingness to shake them off and move forward, to cling to them as comfort blankets rather than to embrace change.

I am aware that the push and pull that I describe in the macrocosm also occurs in the microcosm. It is taking place inside all of us. It can be painful and confusing; it can cause cognitive dissonance. On a daily basis, I often find myself in a butterfly soup of ideas. I find myself oscillating between the sexist spectres of ideas inherited from my parents' generation and the fresh buds of new thinking. But I want to head towards the new, support the youth, embrace the change. We cannot go backward; the change feels too seismic for that.

The question is: how to move forward?

# XIII

Perhaps comedian Dave Chappelle has the answer. He has suggested that we set up councils, similar to those used in the aftermath of oppressive regimes. 'The end of apartheid should have been a fucking bloodbath by any metric in human history, and it wasn't,' he points out. He cites Desmond Tutu and Nelson Mandela as being smart figures who recognized the people as cogs caught up in the corrupt system, incentivized by it, not criminals but victims, and therefore 'the system itself must be tried'. But, he concludes, the only way we can work out what that system is, is if everyone is honest about their role in it.

In South Africa, the Truth and Reconciliation Commission was a justice body, established in 1995, to help heal the country. Its emphasis was not on retributive justice (like the Nuremberg trials) but on restorative justice; not on prosecution but on encouraging dialogue, gathering evidence and information. It allowed victims and perpetrators to tell their stories; a panel then decided if amnesty was justified. This process enabled victims to know that what they had been through was real, having suffered a sense of unreality that those who have been gaslit feel.

Chappelle's idea has potential. But some might ask if such councils could thrive during a time when social media is so punitive and censorious, with an impulse towards oversimplifying complex issues. Detractors of #MeToo argue that our current 'snowflake culture' is too knee-jerk, too witch-hunty, to allow an honest conversation about these important issues. Though I disagree with this viewpoint, I understand the fear that motivates the concern. One wrongly worded tweet or Facebook post can topple a public figure or lead to a worker being fired from their job. I do not believe that 'snowflakes' exist only on the left – they are a phenomenon of all political shades. We cancel obnoxious figures when we should allow them to embarrass themselves in public and let interviewers highlight their abhorrent beliefs, instead of glamorizing them by giving them the allure of the forbidden. It is far better to allow alt-right speakers to express their misogyny openly and dismantle that in a debate than for people to discover their pernicious YouTube videos without a counterargument.

Social media has created a polarizing mentality, exacerbated by the design of communication sites. Those who tweet the most extreme opinions are rewarded with the most likes and retweets. It also creates a culture of virtue-signalling, giving rise to chauvo-feminism. A man can easily convey a sense of being a feminist – and even convince himself that he is one – with a few right-on tweets, without really examining his own principles.

In 2014, Mona Gable wrote a long-form essay in *Los Angeles Magazine* on Hugo Schwyzer, a professor of history and gender studies at Pasadena City College. Hugely successful and popular, he wrote for various feminist websites such as *Jezebel* and *The Frisky* and was celebrated as 'one of LA's most prominent feminists'. But it transpired that his feminism was performative. Gradually, as more details of the gap between his life and his persona began to emerge, he became known as 'a bad-boy feminist' and attracted increasing ire.

In August 2013, he stopped taking his bipolar medication and began tweeting of his double life – i.e., that of a chauvo-feminist. He confessed that 'I secretly wanted to be THE male feminist', but it was 'part of my game'. He said that he used his persona sexually. He had affairs. He slept with porn stars whom he met through his classes. He slept with students. He encouraged those who took his Women in American Society class to keep journals about their feelings, which he then used to suss out young women whom he could have sex with. One of his concluding tweets was: 'You can denounce me now, I'm out of feminism, not because I don't believe in it, but because I'm such a p\*\*\*poor [*sic*] example of it.' Following his breakdown, he ended up in a mental-health facility.

I have such mixed feelings in my response to this story. Schwyzer has defended himself in the comments below the *Los Angeles Magazine* article, saying that he was unfairly depicted as an 'evil person' rather than an 'ill person'. One part of me admires Schwyzer for his honesty, even if it was prompted by meltdown, by a loss of sanity, rather than a reasoned apology.

In another interview, with the *Telegraph*, Schwyzer revealed, 'The serious sort of feminists I grew up with would have looked at what I was writing and would have said it was frivolous. My mother [was] a classic second-wave feminist when I was growing up. She was very disappointed in the direction my feminism took. She wanted me to be writing about wage equality and things like that. It wasn't that I didn't believe in that, but it wasn't sexy enough.' He ended up writing pieces that attracted the most clicks: hence his social media persona fed his polemic, rather than true conviction.

The danger of a society that embraces censorship and the cancel culture is that the resulting collective repression also feeds into the nightmares of our current politics. People end up being drawn to figures such as Trump or Boris Johnson with the mistaken belief that they are being 'honest' or 'telling it like it is'. They are lionized as men who are allowed to speak freely. In fact, Trump's politics and opinions vacillate all over the place, so we can never know if his dreadful opinions are 'honest'; given the contradictions, it seems more likely that he is merely pandering to a mob, appealing to the basest instincts in his supporters, and then inflaming those instincts further. The catch-22 for any leader or alt-right speaker playing this game is that they then suffer a pressure to become increasingly theatrically offensive or extreme in order to maintain their power, thus also debasing themselves. But we could help to dismantle the power of these leaders if we were to allow honest discussion about the problems and prejudices facing society.

# XIV

Here is Helen Lewis on #MeToo: 'it is striking that many of the women I have talked to about their experiences don't want the men who wronged them to face a trial, or losing [*sic*] their job, or even a social media shaming. What most of them want is an acknowledgement – that it did happen, that they are not mad – and an apology.'

And then it happened to me: R apologized.

A quasi, flimsy, dubious apology. The conversation confirmed my worst expectations. I believe that the impulse behind it was sincere, that R truly did want to make amends, but he had processed the problem in his mind by rewriting the narrative and casting himself as a hero and me as a fraught, confused woman. He said that he could not understand why I was upset with him or what he had ever done wrong. The subtext was: *it's all your fault.*

A week later, I met up with a man who cheerfully informed me that he had intended to offer me a prestigious freelancing job but that R had persuaded him out of it, by saying I would be far too busy and uninterested.

I became anxious after that: nightmares became playgrounds of paranoia. How much damage could he wreak on my career, through whispers and insinuations, all done so casually and insidiously? My memoir was coming out the following year and I was both optimistic about, and nervous of, publication. I dreaded him reading it, scouring my personal life for possible ammunition; I feared, too, that he would engineer a bad review, coaxing a newly formed contact into doing this for him.

On the surface, we were apparently 'fine' again. I realized that nothing was ever going to change between us, whether we feigned friendship or overtly engaged in conflict. Nothing I could do could fix it.

But sometimes an honest conversation online – the exchange of accusation and contrition – can lead to genuine reconciliation. Consider the case of Dan Harmon.

Dan Harmon was accused of sexual harassment by Megan Ganz in early January 2018. He had been her boss, a showrunner on NBC's *Community*; she was one of his team of writers. She called him out on Twitter, and he responded with a tweet of shame and apology. At first, Ganz wasn't satisfied. She replied:

It took me years to believe in my talents again, to trust a boss when he complimented me and not cringe when he asked for my number. I was afraid to be enthusiastic, knowing it might be turned against me later.

But a week later, Ganz tweeted a link to Dan's podcast, *Harmontown*:

Please listen to it. It's only seven minutes long, but it is a masterclass in How to Apologize. He's not rationalizing or justifying or making excuses. He doesn't just vaguely acknowledge some general wrongdoing in the past. He gives a full account.

Dan fessed up to the fact that he had been attracted to Ganz and pissed off when he was rejected by her, which led to his abusive behaviour:

I crushed on her and resented her for not reciprocating it, and the entire time I was the one writing her paychecks and in control of whether she stayed or went, and whether she felt good about herself or not, and said horrible things. Just treated her cruelly, pointedly, things I would never, ever would have done if she had been male…

He also confessed, with admirable transparency:

I certainly wouldn't have been able to do it if I had any respect for women. On a fundamental level, I was thinking about them as different creatures. I was thinking about the ones that I liked as having some special role in my life and I did it all by not thinking about it. So, I just want to say, in addition to obviously being sorry, but that's really not the important thing, I want to say I did it by not thinking about it and I got away with it by not thinking about it.

Ganz also tweeted that she was surprised by 'the relief [I felt] feel just hearing him say these things actually happened. I didn't dream it. I'm not crazy.' That was a relief that I recognized.

Ganz concluded their discussion with the tweet:

This was never about vengeance; it's about vindication. That's why it didn't feel right to just accept his apology in private (although I did that, too). Because if any part of this process should be done in the light, it's the forgiveness part. And so, @danharmon, I forgive you.

Those who say that #MeToo is a movement that lacks nuance should note that we can generally sniff out when an apology is real and when it is false. Aziz Ansari was outed after his disastrous date, and after an initial apology, he came back a year later with a Netflix special where he discussed his experience with honesty, grace and humour. During his set, he said, 'It's made not just me but other people more thoughtful,' citing how his friend got in touch and said the article had 'made me think about every date I've ever been on'.

On the other hand, Weinstein's reactions to the accusations against him are not terribly convincing. He has said that he has sought counselling, that he is learning and that people 'make mistakes'. But he still asserts that the sex he had was consensual.

John Hockenberry, who left New York Public Radio after accusations of harassment, wrote a lengthy article in *Harper's*, which gives an interesting insight into a man still processing his shock over a changed cultural climate. He felt that he had been fired as an 'over-correction' in society and was really a 'misguided romantic'. The piece includes an odd digression about how *Lolita* would never have been published if it was submitted today, forgetting that Nabokov actually had a very hard time getting the book published back in 1954, with many US publishers uneasily turning it down. Nabokov himself sent it out under a pen-name and feared he would be fired from his position at Cornell University. He saw *Lolita* as 'a tragedy' – the novel is a subtle and complex exploration of the psyche of a damaged criminal, not a celebration of paedophilia.

Still, one hopes that Weinstein will get to a place of wisdom eventually; that Hockenberry might write a more thoughtful article for *Harper's* next time. We hope and remain patient because none of us is perfect, and our thinking changes slowly, on a daily basis; I know that mine has, hour by hour, in the process of writing and researching this book. There are certainly times in my life when I have made mistakes, been a bad feminist, thoughtless in relationships. I look back on some periods of my life and cringe.

'We're all shitty people,' Aziz Ansari muses in his Netflix set, with superb tragicomedy, 'we're all on a journey. In fifty years we're all going to look back and consider ourselves complete arseholes.'

# XV

And what of men? Many men also came forward during #MeToo, sharing their tales of abuse. What do they think of the aftermath of #MeToo?

Many men have reacted to the movement with maturity, intelligence and grace. For every disappointing response to #MeToo, there is an encouraging one. For every troll, there is a hero.

On 16 October 2017, the day after the #MeToo internet crescendo, Benjamin Law, an Australian journalist and film-maker, created the #HowIWillChange hashtag. Law declared that he would create change by donating regularly to a local women's shelter and calling out sexism and harassment when he saw it happening. And, 'I'll do all this without expecting to be congratulated or praised since women do the heavy lifting every other fucking day.' It was taken up by men across the world. The actor Mark Ruffalo responded with, 'I will never Cat call a woman again. Growing up we were taught

from watching movies that a cat call was a compliment.
I would do it to friends and girlfriends... Not cool. Not a
compliment. Gross. #HowIWillChange.' Jesse T. Smith
tweeted, 'I will keep showing my 3 sons and one grandson how to honor & respect women. Guys – meaningful
change starts in the home.'

Man Enough is a channel on YouTube set up by
Justin Baldoni where men chat with intelligence and
verve about the implications of #MeToo and modern
masculinity. They are heart-warming and inspiring to
watch. In his '#MeToo' video, a table of six men discuss the challenges and how to move forward. Baldoni
considers how he grew up in a society that championed
'bros before hoes', and Tony Porter philosophizes about
a culture of enablers: 'We are defined as good men. We
can wear that tag as long as we're not hurting anyone;
we can stand by and see atrocities happen and not
intervene and not challenge that behaviour and not
lose any of our status.' We need more men doing this,
and we must celebrate and encourage them.

The #MeToo movement has also led men to reflect
on behavioural norms that they might have grown up
with. The *New York Times* questioned a range of men,
asking for their responses to an essay by George Yancy,
a professor at Emory University, entitled '#IAmSexist'.
One man, reflecting on his behaviour of the past
seventy years, said that 'The message is: we are entitled to all the sex we can get and are duty-bound to

pursue it; it is up to women to stop us... we need to teach boys the lessons of Mr Yancy's article from an early age.'

I know the flaw in my argument: what's to say that all of the above men are chauvo-feminists, all style and no substance? To which I'd reply: I can't be sure; none of us can be sure. Tweets are written for audiences, are inherently performative in nature; they are our modern equivalent of the social custom of turning up to church on a Sunday, where you showed your faith as well as experiencing it, where gossip was shared after the service. But the Man Enough channel and George Yancy's essay displayed intelligence and maturity. And time will shake out the chauvo-feminists as the gap between their principles and actions diverge too greatly...

I also sought out personal responses to #MeToo from male friends, feeling that they would give me their honest opinion rather than telling me what I wanted to hear. Below is the transcript of a conversation between me and a male friend; we had dinner, and, as the wine flowed, he opened up and shared his thoughts...

> HIM: As far as men are concerned, there's this underlying suspicion that #MeToo and harassment only applies to ugly men.
>
> ME: Go on...

HIM: If your boss is good-looking and he hits on you, that's fine. But if he's not, then he's in trouble. #MeToo is just an attack on creeps…

ME: But it's too simplistic to reduce it to the issue of looks – when it comes to your boss, it's also about power. Naomi Wolf pointed out some years ago that Harold Bloom's harassment would not be offensive on a date – 'an unwanted hand on a thigh from a date was nothing'. For her, it was the power gap between them – and the abuse of that power – that was particularly troubling. Say a woman starts a new job and her boss is tall, dark and handsome, and then she has a fling with him, and she finds out he's actually a bit of a bastard and it's over. And then he wants to carry on sleeping with her… At that point, he has the power to ignore her for that promotion if she fails to comply.

HIM: The result is, though, that workplace relation-ships will become impossible.

ME: Maybe that's not such a bad thing – after all, most dating now ends up being online. It's much more unusual to hang out in a pub and get chatted up than it used to be. So maybe it's also inevitable that residual dating that might once have taken place in the workplace might shift to the net.

HIM: I have a friend in the film industry who's spoken about how the atmosphere has changed.

Normally there'd be a family atmosphere, everyone would greet each other by hugging each other. But on his last shoot, it was all very terse and formal. People were wary of even going out for drinks at the end of the day, in case something happened – even a flirtation – that's then deemed transgressive, inappropriate, harassment.

ME: I think we're still in a shell-shocked state and things will shift and then, hopefully, settle without sliding backward, as often seems to happen. I mean, the #MeToo experience has occurred before. It happened with Anita Hill thirty years ago, accusing Clarence Thomas, and a slew of sexual-harassment stories emerged in the aftermath. So we have been here before…

HIM: Overall, I'm not convinced that men are really buying into #MeToo deep down. Men want to sleep with women, so now they have to adopt this new position and they'll go along with it just so they can get laid and have relationships.

ME: But there are also women who want to sleep with men, don't forget! Maybe I am being hopelessly naïve, but I have met men who I do feel want to genuinely engage with the new culture. Because they have to. In order to be able to have fulfilling relationships and thrive in the workplace, they can't ignore it, they have to take it on board, and not just as a performative exercise, because that isn't sustainable. I know there are cases of male bosses dodging the issue by not hiring attractive women, but that's no long-term solution, because eventually they'll just be guilty of sexual discrimination instead of sexual harassment. It's just the exchange of one misdemeanour for another.

HIM: The trouble with the whole new scenario is that an extreme crazy vengeful type can now use sexual harassment as a way of attacking someone. There will always be those people.

ME: Unfortunately, it is true that there will always be some rotten apples, yes. But you can't dismantle something largely positive due to the fact that a few people abuse the system. That argument reminds me of discussions on the welfare state, where the public overestimates benefit fraud by a huge degree – they think thirty-four times more benefit money is claimed fraudulently than is. I think that due process is important, and within companies clear guidelines should be laid down so everyone knows where they are. But studies show men and women *do* understand the lines of harassment and they understand it well, so it's not such a blurry situation as some make out. The other issue at stake here is that #MeToo will also protect men. Forty per cent of women say they've been abused, 18 per cent of men. In the future, when more women are in power, male employees will also benefit from a safer workplace.

HIM: Yes, but I still don't think it's fair that if ten years ago a guy put a hand on a woman's knee he gets fired today.

ME: I don't know of any case that extreme happening, but I would agree that it's unfair. But has that happened? If you look into the details of cases such as Roger Ailes, Weinstein, Bill Cosby, there was a lot more going on than that, and that's an understatement.

HIM: Women tend to be more passive on dates, that's the thing, and men have always been expected to make a move. Would you get offended if you went on a date and someone put his hand on your knee?

ME: Probably not. It depends on the context and situation. If I'd been on a date for a few hours and we were getting on well, then no, I wouldn't be offended. Of course, I realize the 'getting on well' is subjective. But, to echo Wolf, I think a hand on a knee on a date is very different from a hand on a knee from your boss or professor. On a date, I'd be fine with it.

HIM: I think that, on a date, a hand on a knee is a question. It's intended to ask a woman if she desires him and wants more. She has a right to remove it. But it wouldn't be right for her to call that a violent act or frame it as abuse.

ME: I agree.

HIM: The other complication to this issue is that women are turned on by powerful men.

ME: That's too simplistic. I don't disagree with the idea that powerful, wealthy men are attractive. But it would be wrong to imagine that this is the only criterion of desirability, particularly in societies where many women are wage earners and we are, thankfully, not necessarily dependent on men to pay the bills. A man can be wealthy and powerful but turn out to be an arsehole. Relationships are also based on communication, respect, understanding. A powerful, wealthy man would only interest me if he was also compassionate, thoughtful and intelligent.

HIM: But if the idea of dating your boss is no longer attractive, women are still excited by the idea of a sexy boss – perhaps someone else's boss. Look at the success of *Fifty Shades of Grey*.

ME: Ha! Yes, I've seen a couple of male right-wing commentators say *Fifty Shades of Grey* proves you do all want to be dominated and harassed deep down, which contradicts #MeToo. That's not so.

HIM: But you're a fan of the books.

ME: I'm not a 'fan', but I did enjoy them and I'll happily admit that. Does it make me a bad feminist?

No – because they're trashy, fun and fantasy. It irritated me when some female campaigners said we should burn the books because they might indoctrinate women into fancying abusive men. It's patronizing and it goes back a long way, that tradition of advising what women should be allowed to read because of their so-called impressionable minds. We don't say that we should burn crime novels in case they give men – traditionally more prone to violence – inspiration to commit murder. We give men the credit for being able to separate fantasy and life, so why suggest women aren't capable of that? I think people can make a distinction between real life and fantasy – though there are complex issues here around life mirroring art and art mirroring life…

HIM: But if these books are all about a secret female fantasy, isn't that still a problem?

ME: I think some men are looking at this issue too simplistically and then making sweeping generalizations about what women want as a result. They imagine we want to return to men dominating women, and that's not true. I had a male friend whose fetish was being dominated by a woman. And he'd always make the point about hugely successful male CEOs whose sexual fetish is being whipped by a dominatrix because they're so burdened by responsibility in their daily lives that they seek submission in their private lives. We're happy for men to have those paradoxes in their lives; we allow them to be complex.

HIM: In that case, you could regard *Fifty Shades* as a reaction to women in the workplace having more power and therefore finding relief in sexual submission, like judges who enjoy being in nappies in their private lives. I once dated a girl who was on the BDSM scene. She was an Oxford graduate and a magazine editor. She told me that she liked to play out darker themes in role play in order to keep them out of her normal life.

ME: Indeed, the point is a fetish can be complex, a part of you that is compartmentalized from your daily life.

\*

Take a look at any article on toxic masculinity and scroll down to the comments underneath. They'll most probably be negative. They will appear to have been written by men, though given the anonymity of the internet, this is not a certainty. In a piece that I read about the need for men to listen to female experiences of #MeToo, published in the *Independent* on 20 October 2018, one accusation was that the piece was 'misandrist'. Another *Independent* piece, which explored male violence as a product of toxic masculinity, resulted in hundreds of outraged comments, with some declaring it 'hate speech'. Many responded with such emotion to the article that they disputed over arguments that were not even in the piece. While you could simply brush all the comments off as the work of trolls, I'm not so sure. Many of the respondents, I felt, looked like ordinary men who were reacting to the current shifts in society in an atmosphere of fear, anger, confusion and panic.

The challenge of the #MeToo movement is that it has redefined what it is to be civilized, but during an era of disillusionment, when people are less invested in society, when both men and women are suffering the effects of austerity and life is not easy for anyone. The fear of losing your job because you've made a misstep must be dominant in some men's minds. As Dave Chappelle says, 'You got all the bad guys scared, and that's good. But the minute they're not scared anymore, it will get worse than it was before. Fear does not make lasting peace.'

In this respect, I agree with Meghan Daum: the #MeToo movement should not become a vehicle for misandry. You cannot fight hate with hate. Men should not be demonized, which only results in their alienation and backlash. We are fighting for equality, not for the oppressed to become oppressors.

Women cannot push forward the change they want on their own. We need men to join us. It means that we need to employ two weapons in our arsenal: that of anger and that of love.

Anger can be a powerful tool. We should be angry, given the statistics, given that one in three women will suffer physical or sexual violence at some point in their lives; that two women in the UK die every day from domestic violence; that the leading cause of death for a pregnant woman in the US is homicide. When the suffragettes were fighting to achieve the vote, they built on the failed efforts of the suffragists, who had demanded the vote using peaceful and reasoned tactics. When this failed, the suffragettes resorted to aggression and military strategy. But one key difference between now and then is that we live in an age of anger, where outrage is the standard currency of Twitter. Sometimes such a surfeit of rage can be exhausting. Sometimes the weapons of love and patience can be refreshing in their contrast. As bell hooks writes:

> If we cannot heal what we cannot feel, by supporting male patriarchal culture that socializes men to deny their feelings, we doom them to live in states of emotional numbness… Only a revolution of values in our nation will end male violence, and that revolution will necessarily be based on a love ethic. To create loving men, we must love males. Loving maleness is different from praising and rewarding males for living up to sexist-defined notions of male identity.

William H. Macy, speaking to press backstage at the Screen Actors Guild Awards, said, 'It's hard to be a man these days. I feel like a lot of us feel like we're under attack and we need to apologize. And maybe we are, and maybe we do.' Shaking things up is a positive, forcing us all to rethink our attitudes and behaviour, but at the same time we need men to act out of empathy rather than fear and anxiety, to move forward with us. They need to be part of the conversation.

In a recent collaboration between GQ and Glamour magazine, where over 1,000 men were surveyed about the #MeToo movement, the results were generally positive, showing that the majority of men did feel that consent was a serious issue, but many were concerned as to where those lines fell. Benjy Hansen-Bundy mused that 'I think guys are still a little wary. One guy wrote, "The movement doesn't come across as inclusive to men." To be honest, I feel some of that trepidation too.' A third of men aged between eighteen and fifty-five said that they were worried of being wrongly accused of sexual harassment at work (though that figure was, interestingly, far lower for men earning over $100,000).

Indeed, some men who hold more privileged positions in society have been slower to adapt to the shifts in power. In the survey I cited above, 41 per cent of men interviewed had never even heard of the #MeToo movement. The men in this category of alarming ignorance were more likely to be young, married, working at an executive level and earning over $100,000.

There are people who worry that #MeToo will emasculate men, that it is the will of women to reduce men to pathetic apologists, shoulders rounded, staring at the floor, without rights or power. Nothing could be further from the truth. Confident men are attractive; confidence only becomes a problem when it veers into cockiness. Power is attractive, too, but it is possible to be powerful and kind. We are simply asking men with power to use it responsibly rather than as a means to dominate and control. We are asking them to grow and be the best versions of themselves.

# XVI

When I was at school, we discussed how to defend ourselves against a leaping-from-the-bushes rapist, but never the issue of consent. My mother gave me a talk about periods, but not once did she ever speak about sex. Once, when I was about nine years old, a boy came to play and kept trying to lock me in the bathroom to play doctors and nurses. I had no idea of what he was trying to do, but my mother kept physically pushing him away from me; what happened remained undiscussed.

Laurie Halse Anderson is the author of the novel *Speak*, about a teenage girl being raped and the aftermath of that violence and its effects on her. Her book is often studied in high schools, and she has toured the US giving talks. She observed that girls listened and connected with her story, sometimes approaching her to ask for help because they had been through a similar experience. With boys, it was a different story. For the past twenty years, she has heard the same thing over and over: that they didn't believe that the protagonist of her story was actually raped. 'They argue that she drank beer, she danced with her attacker and, therefore, she wanted sex. They see his violence as a reasonable outcome. Many of them have clearly been in the same situation.'

She explained that the boys were open about this, not ashamed, and that they were also confused as to why the rape victim was so upset about her experience when it only lasted a few minutes. 'When a boy says these things, the girls in the class are shocked, and the teacher is appalled. They are stunned to discover how many of the guys don't have a clue. So was I, at first. But I quickly learned that reacting with anger and judgment did not help anyone.' Laurie described how she would educate them by presenting statistics that demonstrate the long-term impact of rape and the post-traumatic stress disorder that can result.

Ralph Jones, writing in the *Telegraph*, reports that young men feel angst-ridden and are 'looking for guidance or reassurance on how to be a man in a post #MeToo world'. That education should begin at a young age. Alyssa Milano pointed out 'my kid in school learns that if his clothes catch on fire he should stop, drop and roll. But there's nothing teaching our kids in school about the protocol of gender equality and what that means and decency and respect towards the opposite gender.' The education needs to take place at home and at school. Tony Porter pledged in the Man Enough video discussion that he would fine-tune his son's thinking on a daily basis.

Let the issue be discussed in schools. Let boys and girls have a regular class in which they debate the issue without fear, without censorship, but with honesty, untangling all the messy nuances and complications. You cannot lay down a strict set of rules for courtship, but you can train people to be thoughtful and considerate. Let girls become empowered and men become responsible.

I don't know how to conclude the story of my experiences with R. Truly, I don't know whether it ought to end on a note of pessimism or optimism.

The pessimist in me feels unconvinced that R has changed, despite some promising anecdotes that I've heard from his friends. And, on a wider front, I worry that if sexual harassment is not just about desire but about power, whereby sex is a vehicle for domination and control, then abusive behaviour will simply mutate and adapt. That the means will no longer be a hand on a knee as a way of implying threat but more subtle and insidious forms of coercion. At the beginning of this essay, I asserted that my story was not a #MeToo tale because it did not involve sexual assault or transgression. But what if my story is the #MeToo trend of the future? Just as abusers have co-opted feminism as a shield, then perhaps they will resort to more psychological means, to whisper networks, and if men are now refusing to book business trips with women, or mentor them, or hire them if they are attractive, then perhaps that is just another way to 'other' them and belittle them and stall their power in the workplace. The pessimist thinks of Weinstein calling up Peter Jackson and suggesting that he might not want to hire Ashley Judd or Mira Sorvino for *The Lord of the Rings* because they were 'difficult', which Jackson has cited was part of a 'smear' campaign against two actresses who rejected Weinstein's advances. Maybe R will still carry on doing the same to me...

But the optimist in me reminds me that R is not a monster. He has many good qualities. That the last time I saw him – just before he left for the USA to begin the new semester – he made an effort to be polite and courteous and cautious, as though it was finally dawning on him that I might have a legitimate reason to be angry with him. I consider an anecdote that a mutual friend told me: R related he'd co-hosted a party and spent most of his time making sure that his female guests were not being harassed by men. It is hard to know if this is sincere or smokescreen. But I sense that R is gaining awareness, alertness, that the way he treated women was no longer cool or acceptable in our current era. And he should be given space to repent and reform, and allowed some understanding for his mistakes of the past, given that he was a victim too: the victim of a society that assured him it was fine for him to deal with his pain by taking it out on the women around him.

I think back to the young girl he had fallen out with over her refusal to sleep with him. I consider how that might have panned out, pre-#MeToo. She might have ended up feeling pressurized into going along with it, fearing career repercussions. And R, having pulled off such a feat, might have felt emboldened to treat the next girl he met with a little more psychological pressure. I feel that my response, and the wider shifts in attitude, interrupted his actions. Created an ellipsis. Some sort of victory has been won, not just for the women but for him too. Because I did not want to see R reaching that point where it all caught up with him, where life gave him an almighty slap, where he would be faced with a lifetime of regret and haunted by ghosts.

#MeToo is a kindness not only for women and men but for all the potential abusers who have been stopped in their tracks.

#MeToo has a long, long way to go. In a 2018 survey for Young Women's Trust, a quarter of the women interviewed said that they would be reluctant to report harassment for fear of losing their job. It has still to reach many parts of the globe – in a 2018 survey by Women for Women International, not a single woman in Nigeria or Afghanistan had ever heard of the #MeToo movement. In France, 93 per cent of complaints against sexual harassment are dropped or never followed up by law enforcement.

One day, decades in the future, when we look back to #MeToo, we will consider it to be such a clear-cut issue, just as we do when we look back at the suffragettes. The past is black and white, the present confusing. It seems so obvious to us that they were fighting for the right thing, but at the time I have no doubt it felt as messy to them as #MeToo does to us. Mess is fine; order will emerge from the chaos; new laws and new attitudes will be forged as we move forward.

There have been so many positive outcomes, too:

On 24 February 2020, Harvey Weinstein was sentenced to twenty-three years in prison by Judge James Burke at the New York County Supreme Court, for a first-degree criminal sex act and third-degree rape of a woman. A district attorney in Los Angeles has begun extradition proceedings to bring him to face two further charges.

After Brock Turner was sentenced to just six months for raping Chanel Miller (and let out after three), former California governor Jerry Brown signed two bills inspired by the case. They created mandatory prison sentences for anyone convicted of a similar crime, and the definition of rape was expanded to include other definitions of penetration.

Aaron Persky, the judge who sentenced Turner, was recalled by voters in June 2018 – making him the first California jurist recalled from the bench since 1932. In September 2018, California banned silence clauses in cases involving sexual harassment.

In Tel Aviv, a new programme has been introduced to deal with domestic abuse. Usually in such cases, women and children would have to go to a shelter to escape an abusive partner. Now abusers are sent to a facility for four months. They are the ones who have to transform and make the change.

In Greece, the criminal code has been amended to recognize in law that sex without consent is rape (though a number of European countries still need to catch up…).

The social activism group A Call to Men, which promotes healthy, respectful ways of being a man, has noticed a significant increase in enquiries, as have groups such as 1in6, which helps male survivors of abuse. Men are feeling more able to come forward and be honest about what were previously taboo subjects.

Brett Kavanaugh might have been nominated to the Supreme Court, but Christine Blasey Ford's courage in coming forward is not without benefit. There has been a change in the psyche of the nation. Nearly 60 per cent of voters thought that Kavanaugh lied under oath. And 50 per cent said that the hearings had made them think more about the fact that men have more power in government than women. In a later survey by Perry Undem, 49 per cent of voters said that they wanted more women elected as a result of Kavanaugh's appointment.

Just as the suffrage movement was always about more than just votes for women, likewise the #MeToo movement has expanded to issues beyond the confession of sexual assault. In examining *why* assault happens, it has created a significant shift in cultural awareness. It is about imbalances of power. It is about social structures. It is about gender inequality in the boardroom. It is about the way women have been seen in the world. It is about the way men are brought up to see women. It is about respect and equality. As Tarana Burke first defined #MeToo, it is about 'empowerment through empathy'. It need not be a war between the sexes – it should be a negotiation.

Back in 1997, I witnessed the chauvinism of a male student mocking a female tutor because he felt feminism had nothing to teach him. He did not want to expand his heart nor his mind to consider the female experience. #MeToo has demanded that men do exactly that. As Dan Harmon says, having gained wisdom from the abuse he apologized for: 'The last and most important thing I can say is just think about it. No matter who you are at work, no matter where you work, in what field you're in, no matter what position you have over, under, or side by side with somebody, just think about it.'

'What are women now?' a #MeToo sceptic has asked. To which I would give the simple reply: 'We're human beings.' Both men and women are subtle, complex, nuanced beings. We rarely fit into the boxes of gender stereotypes, which mostly work to stifle and constrain us. We are all worthy of love, respect and equal rights.

# PERMISSIONS

With thanks to Bloomsbury publisher for permission to quote from © Douglas Murray, 2019, *The Madness of Crowds: Gender, Race and Identity*, Continuum, an imprint of Bloomsbury Publishing Plc.

# NOTES

p. 17 **And it was an era in which – as Natasha Walter explores in *Living Dolls*...** Natasha Walter, *Living Dolls: The Return of Sexism*, Virago Press: London (2010)

p. 18 **It's no surprise that a generation of women...** Kira Cochrane, *All the Rebel Women: The Rise of the Fourth Wave of Feminism*, Guardian Books: London (2013)

p. 20 **'the brave women and men who spoke up about the sexual harassment they had endured at the hands of powerful men'...** Jane Mayer and Ronan Farrow, 'Four Women Accuse New York's Attorney General of Physical Abuse', *The New Yorker* (7 May 2018), https://www.newyorker.com/news/news-desk/four-women-accuse-new-yorks-attorney-general-of-physical-abuse

p. 20 **You cannot be a champion of women when you are hitting them...** Ibid.

p. 21 **'show me your breasts' with the warning '*Do you know who I am?*...** Donald Clarke, 'Harvey Weinstein: "I Can Make or Break Your Career. So Show Me Your Breasts"' (2 Sep. 2019), https://www.irishtimes.com/culture/tv-radio-web/harvey-weinstein-i-can-make-or-break-your-career-so-show-me-your-breasts-1.4005037

p. 21 'You're putting your money towards protecting yourself, positioning yourself as a feminist, as an ally to powerful women.' She concluded in angry resignation: 'Nobody was ever going to win against this guy... From an interview with Rebecca Traister, BBC, *Untouchable: The Rise and Fall of Harvey Weinstein*, BBC (25 Jan. 2020)

p. 22 I so respect women... Kate Lonczak, 'Ironically, Harvey Weinstein Set Up a Foundation Last Year to Support Women Directors at USC', *The Tab* (5 Oct. 2017), https://thetab.com/us/usc/2017/10/05/harvey-weinstein-6157

p. 22 'While this might seem coincidental... Ibid.

p. 22 Even Aziz Ansari – billed as the nice guy with a Netflix show... Katie Way, 'I Went on a Date with Aziz Ansari', *Babe* (13 Jan. 2018), https://babe.net/2018/01/13/aziz-ansari-28355

p. 23 I think Venus and Serena have won about four each... Sabrina Barr, 'Andy Murray's 10 Best Feminist Moments', *Independent* (9 Jul. 2019), https://www.independent.co.uk/life-style/women/andy-murray-wimbledon-2019-feminist-moments-equal-pay-sexism-women-serena-williams-a8996971.html

p. 35 condemned by my status to silence and inaction... Pierre Choderlos de Laclos, trans. Douglas Parmée, *Les Liaisons Dangereuses*, Oxford World Classics: Oxford (1998), p. 181

p. 36 'take advantage of her'... Francine Pascal, *Caitlin*, Bantam Books: New York (1998)

p. 39 'Only 7 per cent of Britons call themselves feminists – 9 per cent of women and 4 per cent of men. But 74 per cent of women said that they were sympathetic to feminism. It was the label 'feminism' that women did not like, some fearing it was 'bitchy' or misandrist... Fawcett Society, 'We Are a Nation of Hidden Feminists' (15 Jan. 2016), https://www.fawcettsociety.org.uk/news/we-are-a-nation-of-hidden-feminists

p. 39 Furthermore, a 2018 YouGov poll found that 34 per cent of women said 'yes' when asked if they were a feminist (up from 27 per cent in 2013)... Christina Scharff, 'Why So Many Young Women Don't Call Themselves Feminist', *BBC News* (6 Feb. 2019), https://www.bbc.co.uk/news/uk-politics-47006912

p. 41 **whether you are citing the number of people at your inauguration compared to Obama's...** Jon Swaine, *Guardian* (6 Sep. 2018), https://www.theguardian.com/world/2018/sep/06/donald-trump-inauguration-crowd-size-photos-edited

p. 41 **wielding a Sharpie to plot the fictional path of Hurricane Dorian so that it matches your public statement...** Madeleine Carlisle, 'Newly-Released NOAA Emails Show Anger and Confusion Around Trump's "Doctored" Hurricane Dorian Map', *Time* (1 Feb. 2020), https://time.com/5775953/trump-dorian-alabama-sharpiegate-noaa/

p. 45 **'never conceded the hypocrisy of being out in the world preaching feminist ideals, while at the same time, taking away my right to make choices for my life...** Kai Cole, 'Joss Whedon Is a "Hypocrite Preaching Feminist Ideals," Ex-Wife Kai Cole Says', *TheWrap* (20 Aug. 2017), https://www.thewrap.com/joss-whedon-feminist-hypocrite-infidelity-affairs-ex-wife-kai-cole-says/

p. 46 **'are socialized to doubt themselves and continually apologize for disagreeing [with] or upsetting their partners...** Robin Stern, 'I've Counseled Hundreds of Victims of Gaslighting', *Vox* (3 Jan. 2019), https://www.vox.com/first-person/2018/12/19/18140830/gaslighting-relationships-politics-explained

p. 46 **I watched Claire Foy being interviewed by Graham Norton...** BBC, *The Graham Norton Show* (4 Nov. 2016), https://www.youtube.com/watch?v=lqc-dW76_vM

p. 47 **In the US, women are twice as likely to take them as men...** Abigail Miller, 'Women Are Twice as Likely to Use Antidepressants Compared to Men', *Daily Mail* (15 Aug. 2017), https://www.dailymail.co.uk/health/article-4790490/Women-twice-likely-use-antidepressants-men.html

p. 47 **while the reverse is true for men, whose depression is more likely to be underdetected and undertreated...** L. Thunander Sundbom, K. Bingefors, Kerstin Hedborg and Dag Isacson, 'Are Men Under-Treated and Women Over-Treated With Antidepressants? Findings from a Cross-Sectional Survey in Sweden', *BJPsych Bulletin* (Jun. 2017), https://pubmed.ncbi.nlm.nih.gov/28584650/

p. 48 **Men direct their negative emotions into anger and aggression, while women ruminate on their depression**

**and amplify it...** L. A. Martin, H. W. Neighbors and D. M. Griffith, 'The Experience of Symptoms of Depression in Men vs Women', *JAMA Psychiatry* 70 (Oct. 2013), https://pubmed.ncbi.nlm.nih.gov/23986338/

p. 48 **'the numbers of men who are alcoholic or impulsively violent are added to the numbers who are depressed the total is about the same as the number of women who are depressed...** Daniel Nettle, *Strong Imagination: Madness, Creativity and Human Nature*, Oxford University Press: Oxford (2002), p. 112

p. 48 **A self-confessed gaslighter, a Canadian lawyer called Greg, gave an interview for the BBC...** Megha Mohan, 'Cheating and Manipulation: Confessions of a Gaslighter', *BBC News* (11 Jan. 2018), https://www.bbc.co.uk/news/stories-42460315

p. 48 **The psychologist George K. Simon says that there are two key traits that attract gaslighters, 'conscientiousness' and 'agreeableness'...** Ibid.

p. 49 **'from my experience, it's not true that it is vulnerable or insecure women who are susceptible to gaslighting...** Ibid.

p. 49 **One victim who escaped from such a relationship, Kay Schubach, observed that it is 'very, very common' that 'your self-esteem gets eroded'...** Melissa Davey, 'The Most Dangerous Time', *Guardian* (2 Jun. 2015), https://www.theguardian.com/society/ng-interactive/2015/jun/02/domestic-violence-five-women-tell-their-stories-of-leaving-the-most-dangerous-time

p. 50 **On average, a woman in a bad relationship will endure fifty instances of abuse...** *SafeLives*, 'How Long Do People Live with Domestic Abuse, and When Do They Get Help to Stop It?', *SafeLives*, http://www.safelives.org.uk/policy-evidence/about-domestic-abuse/how-long-do-people-live-domestic-abuse-and-when-do-they-get

p. 50 **50 to 75 per cent of domestic-violence homicides occur at the point of break-up or after she has left her abuser...** Jana Kasperkevic, 'Private Violence: Up to 75% of Abused Women Who Are Murdered Are Killed after They Leave Their Partners', *Guardian* (20 Oct. 2014), https://www.theguardian.com/money/us-money-blog/2014/oct/20/domestic-private-violence-women-men-abuse-hbo-ray-rice

p. 54 **Later, Paltrow found out that he used her as a gaslighting tool...** Jodi Kantor and Megan Twohey, *She Said*, Bloomsbury: London (2019), p. 254

p. 60 **'taking us back to the Victorian archetypes of early silent films, where twirling villains tied damsels in distress to railroad tracks...** Camille Paglia, 'Camille Paglia on Movies, #MeToo and Modern Sexuality', *The Hollywood Reporter* (27 Feb. 2018), https://www.hollywoodreporter.com/news/camille-paglia-movies-metoo-modern-sexuality-endless-bitter-rancor-lies-1088450

p. 60 **'Female emancipation was all about giving women control over their own destinies...** Melanie Phillips, 'MeToo Feminism Is Victim Culture, Not Courage', *The Times* (5 Feb. 2018), https://www.thetimes.co.uk/article/metoo-feminism-is-victim-culture-not-courage-lh0gmd3pn

p. 62 **Paz de la Huerta remarks in *Untouchable*, 'when you read about rape'...** BBC, *Untouchable: The Rise and Fall of Harvey Weinstein*, BBC (25 Jan. 2020)

p. 62 **Do you really want to make an enemy out of me for five minutes of your time?...** Ibid.

p. 62 **three-quarters of European states recognize an assault only when physical violence, threats or coercion are involved...** Andy Gregory, 'Only a Quarter of EU Countries Have Consent-Based Definitions of Rape, Amnesty Reveals', *Independent* (24 Nov. 2018), https://www.independent.co.uk/news/rape-legislation-europe-consent-women-violence-research-amnesty-a8649131.html

p. 65 **Having seen his shows and read excerpts from his dating guide, *Modern Romance*, she wasn't expecting this sort of behaviour from him...** Katie Way, 'I Went on a Date with Aziz Ansari', *Babe* (13 Jan. 2018), https://babe.net/2018/01/13/aziz-ansari-28355

p. 70 **the staff at the *New York Times* had no idea how people would react to the piece, or indeed if anyone would care...** Jodi Kantor and Megan Twohey, *She Said*, Bloomsbury: London (2019), pp. 181–2

p. 70 **Ronan Farrow found there was a lack of support for airing the story from his employers at NBC and so ended up taking it to the *New Yorker* instead...** Rich McHugh,

'"You Are to Stand Down": Ronan Farrow's Producer on How NBC Killed Its Weinstein Story', *Vanity Fair* (11 Oct. 2019), https://www.vanityfair.com/news/2019/10/how-nbc-killed-its-weinstein-story

p. 71 **Michelle Manning Barish explained: 'I was ashamed. For victims, shame played a huge role in most of these stories'...** Jane Mayer and Ronan Farrow, 'Four Women Accuse New York's Attorney General of Physical Abuse', *New Yorker* (7 May 2018), https://www.newyorker.com/news/news-desk/four-women-accuse-new-yorks-attorney-general-of-physical-abuse

p. 71 **'A number of them advised her to keep the story to herself, arguing that Schneiderman was too valuable a politician for the Democrats to lose'...** Ibid.

p. 71 **his ex-wife, Jennifer Cunningham, said that she found it impossible to believe the allegations...** Danny Hakim and Vivian Wang, 'Eric Schneiderman Resigns as New York Attorney General Amid Assault Claims by 4 Women', *New York Times* (7 May 2018), https://www.nytimes.com/2018/05/07/nyregion/new-york-attorney-general-eric-schneiderman-abuse.html

p. 71 **a very common epithet used to describe him is 'charming', and, indeed, one of his male colleagues spoke about having 'survivor guilt'...** BBC, *Untouchable: The Rise and Fall of Harvey Weinstein*, BBC (25 Jan. 2020)

p. 73 **The article, written by Rebecca Traister, made the point that many of the men who were disgraced were seen as complex villains...** Rebecca Traister, 'The Toll of MeToo: Assessing the Costs for Those Who Came Forward', *The Cut* (30 Sep. 2019), https://www.thecut.com/2019/09/the-toll-of-me-too.html

p. 73 **black snitch bitch...** Susan Chira and Catrin Einhorn, 'How Tough Is It to Change a Culture of Harassment?', *New York Times* (19 Dec. 2017), https://www.nytimes.com/interactive/2017/12/19/us/ford-chicago-sexual-harassment.html

p. 73 **'I would never do it again and I would never recommend another woman do it...** Rebecca Traister, 'The Toll of MeToo: Assessing the Costs for Those Who Came Forward', *The Cut* (30 Sep. 2019), https://www.thecut.com/2019/09/the-toll-of-me-too.html

p. 74 **Some of Weinstein's accusers – had Weinstein not had the power to pick up the phone and bad-mouth them, effectively stalling their progress – could have gone on to flourish as great actresses...** Peter Jackson reported that Ashley Judd and Mira Sorvino's careers were derailed by Miramax smearing them as 'difficult women', BBC News, 'Weinstein "Derailed My Career" Sorvino Says after Peter Jackson Claim', *BBC News* (16 Dec. 2017), https://www.bbc.co.uk/news/entertainment-arts-42377607

p. 75 **As Sarah Ditum points out, 'what the government actually cut were women's rights'...** Helen Lewis, 'The Year Women Said: Me Too', *New Statesman* (10 Oct. 2018), https://www.newstatesman.com/politics/feminism/2018/10/year-women-said-me-too

p. 77 **Her compelling argument is that if she speaks out it will be 'the first and last line of your obituary'...** Eliana Dockterman, 'Bombshell Is the Latest Example of Pop Culture Reckoning with the Complicated Reality of #MeToo at Work', *Time* (16 Dec. 2019), https://time.com/5744161/bombshell-succession-the-morning-show-me-too/

p. 78 **When Tarana Burke first created her #MeToo movement, 'Our vision from the beginning was'...** Me Too, 'About', https://metoomvmt.org/about/

p. 78 **Molly Ringwald, in an article for the *New Yorker*...** Molly Ringwald, 'All the Other Harvey Weinsteins', *New Yorker* (17 Oct. 2017), https://www.newyorker.com/culture/cultural-comment/all-the-other-harveys

p. 79 **'What I'm angry about is that there isn't another way. There isn't a system in place...** Lauren O'Connor, 'I Had Nightmares Constantly after the *Times* Story', *New York Magazine* (30 Sep. 2019), https://www.pressreader.com/usa/new-york-magazine/20190930/282827897880440

p. 79 **'I was told that wasn't even worth considering because of the disparity of power...** Holly Watt, 'Harvey Weinstein Aide Tells of "Morally Lacking" Non-Disclosure Deal', *Guardian* (28 Mar. 2018), https://www.theguardian.com/film/2018/mar/28/harvey-weinstein-assistant-zelda-perkins-i-was-trapped-in-a-vortex-of-fear

p. 79 **my naivety was met with hilarity...** Ibid.

p. 79 **Chiu felt unable to approach a trauma counsellor to discuss the rape she'd endured. She suffered depression, attempted suicide and did not even tell her husband what had happened to her...** Hilary Lewis, 'Ex-Weinstein Assistant Opens Up about Alleged Attempted Rape, 20-Year Silence', *Hollywood Reporter* (6 Oct. 2019), https://www.hollywoodreporter.com/news/weinstein-assistant-rowena-chiu-attempted-rape-20-year-silence-1245739

p. 80 **Chanel Miller was sexually assaulted behind a dumpster at a Stanford University fraternity party by Brock Turner when she was a student...** Irin Carmon and Amelia Schonbek, 'Was It Worth It?', *The Cut* (30 Sep. 2019), https://www.thecut.com/2019/09/coming-forward-about-sexual-assault-and-what-comes-after.html

p. 80 **The proportion of rapes prosecuted in England and Wales...** Lizzie Dearden, 'Rape "Decriminalised" as Only 1.4% of Reported Attacks Prosecuted in England and Wales', *Independent* (17 Oct. 2019), https://www.independent.co.uk/news/uk/crime/rape-prosecutions-uk-disclosure-mobile-phones-cps-a9160556.html

p. 81 **The average adult man in England and Wales is more likely to be raped...** Georgina Lee, 'Men Are More Likely to Be Raped Than Be Falsely Accused of Rape', *Channel 4 News* (12 Oct. 2018), https://www.channel4.com/news/factcheck/factcheck-men-are-more-likely-to-be-raped-than-be-falsely-accused-of-rape

p. 82 **Rodger left behind a 140-page manifesto that dripped with bile and misogyny...** Elliot Rodger, *My Twisted World*, https://www.documentcloud.org/documents/1173808-elliot-rodger-manifesto.html

p. 84 **'many of us had weathered more than we had been willing to admit to one another...** Moira Donegan, 'I Started the Media Men List', *The Cut* (10 Jan. 2018), https://www.thecut.com/2018/01/moira-donegan-i-started-the-media-men-list.html

p. 85 **'Abusers have enormous egos...** Jana Kasperkevic, 'Private Violence: Up to 75% of Abused Women Who Are Murdered Are Killed after They Leave Their Partners', *Guardian* (20 Oct. 2014), https://www.theguardian.com/money/us-money-blog/2014/oct/20/domestic-private-violence-women-men-abuse-hbo-ray-rice

p. 92 **'I gained a lot of privileges, I lost a lot of connection...** Thomas Page McBee, interviewed for the Aspen Festival of Ideas (2018), https://www.youtube.com/watch?v=5wTwj w161f0

p. 94 **Darwin made the argument in *On the Origin of Species*. Men, he declared, have the 'unfortunate birthright' of competitiveness...** Charles Darwin, *On the Origin of Species*, Penguin: London (2009)

p. 94 **In 2019, in the UK, 25.3 per cent of girls got top grades of A (or 7) at GCSE, compared to 18.6 per cent of boys in Year 11, at age sixteen...** Richard Adams, Niamh McIntyre and Sally Weale, 'GCSE Results: Girls Fare Better Than Boys under More Rigorous Courses', *Guardian* (22 Aug. 2019), https://www.theguardian.com/education/2019/aug/22/gcse-results-more-rigorous-courses-appear-to-benefit-girls

p. 94 **'alternative dating strategy'...** Ayala Ochert, 'Why Men Want to Rape', *Times Higher Education* (4 Feb. 2000), https://www.timeshighereducation.com/features/why-men-want-to-rape/150003.article

p. 94 **'We fervently believe that, just as the leopard's spots and the giraffe's elongated neck are the result of aeons of past Darwinian selection, so is rape'...** R. Thornhill and C. T. Palmer, 'Why Men Rape', *New York Academy of Sciences* (January/February 2000), https://www.csus.edu/indiv/m/merlinos/thornhill.html

p. 95 **'it is flexible, malleable and changeable...** Robin McKie, 'Male and Female Ability Differences Down to Socialisation, Not Genetics', *Guardian* (15 Aug. 2010), https://www.theguardian.com/world/2010/aug/15/girls-boys-think-same-way

p. 95 **Scientist Lise Eliot also explains that 'All such skills are learned and neuro-plasticity'...** Ibid.

p. 96 **'a rewarding, low-risk act'...** Diana Scully, *Understanding Sexual Violence: A Study of Convicted Rapists*, Routledge: London (1990)

p. 97 **In a 2013 *Lancet* study, 22.7 per cent of men in China admitted to rape...** R. Jewkes, E. Fulu, T. Roselli and C.

Garcia-Moreno, 'Prevalence of and Factors Associated with Non-Partner Rape Perpetration: Findings from the UN Multi-Country Cross-Sectional Study on Men and Violence in Asia and the Pacific', *The Lancet* (10 Sep. 2013), https://www.thelancet.com/journals/langlo/article/PIIS2214-109X%2813%2970069-X/fulltext

p. 97 **The anthropologist Peggy Reeves Sanday has also extensively studied the sociocultural context of rape...** Peggy Reeves Sanday, *Rape-Free versus Rape-Prone: How Culture Makes a Difference*, MIT Press: Cambridge, MA (2003)

p. 97 **'an organized system for abusing women... it's an entire machine, a supply chain' and 'if white men could have a playground, this would be it'...** Jodi Kantor and Megan Twohey, *She Said*, Bloomsbury: London (2019), p. 12

p. 98 **'I always imagined that actresses wanted to sleep with Harvey'...** Rebecca Traister, BBC, *Untouchable: The Rise and Fall of Harvey Weinstein*, BBC (25 Jan. 2020)

p. 98 **there was an underlying assumption that she'd got the part because 'she'd slept with Harvey', never that 'he'd slept with her'...** BBC, *Untouchable: The Rise and Fall of Harvey Weinstein*, BBC (25 Jan. 2020)

p. 98 **Erika Rosenbaum was told by him, 'Everybody does this'...** Ibid.

p. 98 **The *Guardian* gathered a series of statements from women in response to the question 'Was Wolf right to speak out?'...** Laura Barton, 'Who's Crying Wolf?', *Guardian* (26 Feb. 2004), https://www.theguardian.com/world/2004/feb/26/gender.uk

p. 101 **CBS News grouped together a number of successful men (including film-maker Judd Apatow, astronaut Leland D. Melvin and chef Tom Colicchio) to discuss the issue...** CBS *This Morning*, 'Where Do We Go from Here? Industry-Leading Men Weigh in on the Sexual Harassment Epidemic', CBS (14 Dec. 2017), https://www.cbsnews.com/news/men-weigh-in-on-me-too-movement-sexual-harassment-solutions/

p. 102 **Warren Farrell, author of *The Myth of Male Power*, points out that while women can be reduced to 'sex objects'...** Warren Farrell, *The Myth of Male Power*, Simon & Schuster: New York (1993)

p. 102 **The fact is, a lot of men seem to feel their place in the modern world is becoming less purposeful...** Sabrina Barr, 'What Is Toxic Masculinity and How Can It Be Addressed?' *Independent* (17 Jan. 2019), https://www.independent.co.uk/life-style/toxic-masculinity-definition-what-is-boys-men-gillette-ad-behaviour-attitude-girls-women-a8729336.html

p. 102 **Men are far more likely to die from suicide than women...** Helene Schumacher, 'Why More Men Than Women Die by Suicide', BBC (18 Mar. 2019), https://www.bbc.com/future/article/20190313-why-more-men-kill-themselves-than-women

p. 103 **In the US, Canada and Britain, the worst-hit group are middle-aged men, who often suffer in greater numbers...** Samaritans, Suicide Facts and Figures, *Samaritans*, https://www.samaritans.org/about-samaritans/research-policy/suicide-facts-and-figures/

p. 103 **In the UK, 2.5 million men report having no close friends...** John Bingham, '2.5 Million Men "Have No Close Friends"', *Telegraph* (14 Nov. 2015), https://www.telegraph.co.uk/men/active/mens-health/11996473/2.5-million-men-have-no-close-friends.html

p. 103 **Damien Ridge observes that 'Loneliness in older men is a real issue...** Max Liu, 'Is It Just Me... or Does Everyone Lose Their Friends in their 30s?', Max Liu, *Guardian* (7 Nov. 2015), https://www.theguardian.com/society/2015/nov/07/why-men-lose-friends-in-their-30s

p. 103 **A 2015 study shows...** David M. Mayer, 'How Men Get Penalized for Straying from Masculine Norms', *Harvard Business Review* (8 Oct. 2018), https://hbr.org/2018/10/how-men-get-penalized-for-straying-from-masculine-norms

p. 104 **'The way I behaved was hurtful, degrading and infuriating to a degree that I have only begun to understand in the past month'...** Heloise Wood, 'Paris Review Editor Resigns after Internal Investigation', *The Bookseller* (7 Dec. 2017), https://www.thebookseller.com/news/paris-review-editor-resigns-amidst-sexual-allegations-687451

p. 104 **she found the stipulation impossible to enforce...** Jodi Kantor and Megan Twohey, *She Said*, Bloomsbury: London (2019), p. 67

p. 104 **According to Germaine Greer, the #MeToo Movement has infantilized women...** 'Germaine v #MeToo: Women Are Strong, and Not to Be Infantilised', *Sydney Morning Herald* (22 Jan. 2018), https://www.smh.com.au/national/germaine-greer-raises-valid-points-on-metoo-but-sometimes-its-not-that-easy-20180122-h0lzff.html

p. 105 **Hope D'Amore said that she thought Weinstein probably genuinely believed this...** BBC, *Untouchable: The Rise and Fall of Harvey Weinstein*, BBC (25 Jan. 2020)

p. 107 **Ronan Farrow being assured that Rose McGowan's complaints about Weinstein had no substance because 'She's crazy!'...** [Farrow details being told this in Chapter 34 by Lisa Bloom] Ronan Farrow, *Catch and Kill: Lies, Spies and a Conspiracy to Catch Predators*, Fleet: London (2019)

p. 107 **'his career too was dashed to the floor by people high on the octane of unreflective moral outrage'...** Douglas Murray, 'Blurred Lines', *The Spectator* (4 Nov. 2017) https://www.spectator.co.uk/2017/11/the-consequence-of-this-new-sexual-counter-revolution-no-sex-at-all/

p. 108 **women's rights... 'appeared to be reaching some sort of settlement'...** Douglas Murray, *The Madness of Crowds: Gender, Race and Identity*, Bloomsbury Continuum: London (2019)

p. 108 **Yet, in the land of the free, the female right to terminate a pregnancy is reversing, with eleven states restricting abortion rights in 2019...** [Alabama attempted to ban abortion outright, even in cases of rape and incest, but the Bill was temporarily blocked by federal judge US District Judge Myron Thompson.] Annalisa Merelli and Ana Campoy, 'These Are All the States That Have Adopted Anti-Abortion Laws So Far in 2019', *Quartz* (30 May 2019), https://qz.com/1627412/these-are-all-the-states-with-anti-abortion-laws-signed-in-2019/

p. 109 **Feminism has always been forward-looking...** Grayson Perry, *The Descent of Man*, Allen Lane: London (2016), p. 91

p. 109 **Lord Curzon, head of the National League for Opposing Woman Suffrage, argued that 'political activity will tend to take woman away from her proper sphere and highest duty, which is maternity'...** Lord Curzon, *Fifteen Good Reasons Against the Grant of Female Suffrage*, 1912

p. 110 'women have not, as a sex, or a class, the calmness of temperament, or the balance of mind... necessary to qualify them to exercise a weighty judgement in political affairs... Ibid.

p. 110 'a sex rivalry, which has too often masqueraded as reform'... Julia Bush, 'The Anti-Suffrage Movement', *British Library* (5 Mar. 2018), https://www.bl.uk/votes-for-women/articles/the-anti-suffrage-movement

p. 110 Julia Bush has noted: 'In many ways the suffrage and anti-suffrage movements were interdependent... Ibid.

p. 110 'Am I allowed nuanced feelings about #MeToo?'... Meghan Daum, 'Team Older Feminist: Am I Allowed Nuanced Feelings about #MeToo?', *Guardian* (16 Oct. 2019), https://www.theguardian.com/lifeandstyle/2019/oct/16/metoo-older-feminists-problem-with-everything-extract

p. 111 Daum has also argued in a piece for *Medium* that we should not criticize men but instead address our own issues with toxic femininity... Meghan Daum, '#MeToo Will Not Survive Unless We Recognize Toxic Femininity', *Medium* (25 Oct. 2017), https://gen.medium.com/metoo-will-not-survive-unless-we-recognize-toxic-femininity-6e82704ee616

p. 112 hollow sloganeering', for 'its suggestion that women are some monolithic entity... Ibid.

p. 112 Meghan Daum's reaction to the Shitty Media Men list, for example, is one of concern about women complaining about 'a weird lunch'... Ibid.

p. 113 But a recent survey for *Vox* proved the opposite... Anna North, 'Why Women Are Worried about #MeToo', *Vox* (5 Apr. 2018), https://www.vox.com/2018/4/5/17157240/me-too-movement-sexual-harassment-aziz-ansari-accusation

p. 113 Germaine Greer saying that #MeToo is a 'whingeing' movement... Alison Flood, 'Germaine Greer Criticises "Whingeing" #MeToo Movement', *Guardian* (23 Jan. 2018), https://www.theguardian.com/books/2018/jan/23/germaine-greer-criticises-whingeing-metoo-movement

p. 113 'Rape is a daily crime, it's not spectacular. What we need is a coherent law of sexual assault'... Ibid.

p. 113 Daum herself has concluded that the conversation about #MeToo has begun 'to split down generational lines'...

Meghan Daum, *The Problem with Everything: My Journey Through the New Culture Wars*, Gallery Books: New York (2019)

p. 114 **Daum says that she was taught 'If the drunk guy sitting next to you at the wedding reception gets fresh, kick him in the shins'...** Meghan Daum, 'Team Older Feminist: Am I Allowed Nuanced Feelings about #MeToo?', *Guardian* (16 Oct. 2019), https://www.theguardian.com/lifeandstyle/2019/oct/16/metoo-older-feminists-problem-with-everything-extract

p. 115 **'We can no longer ignore that voice within women that says, "I want something more than my husband and my children and my home"'...** Betty Friedan, *The Feminine Mystique*, W. W. Norton: New York (1963)

p. 115 **it's so whiny; it's just enough to drive a modern person mad to listen...** Nellie Bowles, 'Jordan Peterson, Custodian of the Patriarchy', *New York Times* (18 May 2018), https://www.nytimes.com/2018/05/18/style/jordan-peterson-12-rules-for-life.html

p. 115 **Interviewed for his views on the #MeToo movement...** National Post, 'Jordan Peterson on the #MeToo Moment', *National Post* (24 Mar. 2018), https://www.youtube.com/watch?v=g8GSlP2yCD8

p. 117 **'younger men acknowledge the problem, but older men tend to dismiss it as overblown'...** Justine Harman and Benjy Hansen-Bundy, 'What 1,147 Men Really Think About #MeToo', *Glamour* (30 May 2018), https://www.glamour.com/story/men-metoo-survey-glamour-gq

p. 117 **In another survey, conducted by YouGov, it was found that more than a third of over-65s do not regard non-consensual sex in marriage or a relationship as rape...** BBC News, 'Survey Reveals "Alarming" Attitudes of Britons on Rape', *BBC News* (6 Dec. 2018), https://www.bbc.co.uk/news/uk-46460434

p. 117 **And 42 per cent of over-65s said that if sexual activity continues after a woman changes her mind, it is not rape, compared with 22 per cent of the 25–49s...** Ibid.

p. 117 **In Ancient Greece, it was regarded as a greater sin for a man to have consensual sex with another man's wife than** it was for him to rape her... Peter Jones, 'Why the Ancient Greeks thought Adultery Was Worse than Rape', *The Spectator* (25 Oct. 2014), https://www.spectator.co.uk/article/why-the-ancient-greeks-thought-adultery-was-worse-than-rape

p. 117 **Rapists got a doubled fine, while adulterous seducers suffered the death penalty...** Jack Holland, *A Brief History of Misogyny: The World's Oldest Prejudice*, Robinson: London (2012)

p. 118 **'shame that love brings with it is no different from the pain: it is only felt once... The pleasure, however, remains...** Pierre Choderlos de Laclos, trans. Douglas Parmée, *Les Liaisons Dangereuses*, Oxford World Classics: Oxford (1998), p. 250

p. 118 **'Tell me then, languishing lover'** Ibid.

p. 119 **These days, it is often echoed in the internet porn that teenage boys watch...** Antonia Quadara, Alissar El-Murr and Joe Latham, 'The Effects of Pornography on Children and Young People', Australian Institute of Family Studies (Dec. 2017), https://aifs.gov.au/publications/effects-pornography-children-and-young-people-snapshot

p. 121 **'The end of apartheid should have been a fucking bloodbath by any metric in human history, and it wasn't'...** Katie Kilkenny, 'Dave Chappelle Jokes that Louis C.K. Accuser Has a "Brittle Ass Spirit" in Netflix Special', *Hollywood Reporter* (31 Dec. 2017), https://www.hollywoodreporter.com/news/dave-chappelle-jokes-louis-ck-accuser-has-a-brittle-ass-spirit-netflix-special-1070882

p. 123 **In 2014, Mona Gable wrote a long-form essay in *Los Angeles Magazine* on Hugo Schwyzer...** Mona Gable, 'The Hugo Problem', *Los Angeles Magazine* (26 Mar. 2014), https://www.lamag.com/longform/the-hugo-problem/

p. 124 **In another interview, with the *Telegraph*, Schwyzer revealed, 'The serious sort of feminists I grew up with...** Rebecca Holman, 'The Rise and Fall of America's Most Infamous "Male Feminist": Hugo Schwyzer', *Telegraph* (27 Sep. 2013), https://www.telegraph.co.uk/women/womens-life/10338624/The-rise-and-fall-of-Americas-most-infamous-male-feminist-Hugo-Schwyzer.html

p. 126 **'it is striking that many of the women I have talked to about their experiences don't want the men who wronged** them to face a trial... Helen Lewis, 'The Year Women Said: Me Too', *New Statesman* (10 Oct. 2018), https://www.newstatesman.com/politics/feminism/2018/10/year-women-said-me-too

p. 127 **Dan Harmon was accused of sexual harassment by Megan Ganz in early January 2018...** Megan McCluskey, 'Dan Harmon Gives "Full Account" of Sexually Harassing *Community* Writer Megan Ganz', *Time* (11 Jan. 2018), https://time.com/5100019/dan-harmon-megan-ganz-sexual-harassment-apology/

p. 128 **I crushed on her and resented her for not reciprocating it, and the entire time I was the one writing her paychecks...** Drew Schwartz, 'Dan Harmon Explains Exactly How He Harassed a Female "Community" Writer', *Vice* (12 Jan. 2018), https://www.vice.com/en_uk/article/a3nydj/dan-harmon-explains-exactly-how-he-harassed-female-community-writer-vgtrn

p. 130 **During his set, he said, 'It's made not just me but other people more thoughtful'...** Aziz Ansari, *Right Now*, Netflix, first broadcast 9 July 2019

p. 130 **John Hockenberry, who left New York Public Radio after accusations of harassment, wrote a lengthy article in *Harper's*...** John Hockenberry, 'Exile, and a Year of Trying to Find a Road Back from Personal and Public Shame', *Harper's* (Oct. 2018), https://harpers.org/archive/2018/10/exile-4/

p. 131 **We're all shitty people,' Aziz Ansari muses in his Netflix set, with superb tragicomedy...** Aziz Ansari, *Right Now*, Netflix, first broadcast 9 July 2019

p. 132 **On 18 October, the day after the #MeToo internet crescendo, Benjamin Law, an Australian journalist and film-maker, created the #HowIWillChange hashtag...** Alanna Vagianos, 'In Response To #MeToo, Men Are Tweeting #HowIWillChange', *Huffington Post* (19 Oct. 2017), https://www.huffingtonpost.co.uk/entry/in-response-to-metoo-men-are-tweeting-howiwillchange_n_59e79bd3e4b00905bdae455d

p. 132 **'I'll do all this without expecting to be congratulated or praised since women do the heavy lifting every other fucking day...** Ibid.

p. 133 **Mark Ruffalo responded with, 'I will never Cat call a woman again'...** Mark Ruffalo (@markruffalo), 'I will never

Cat call a woman again…' Twitter (19 Oct. 2017), https://twitter.com/markruffalo/status/920805965527523328?lang=en

p. 133 **Jesse T. Smith tweeted, 'I will keep showing my 3 sons and one grandson how to honor & respect women'…** Declan Cashin, 'Men are Using #HowIWillChange to Back the #MeToo Twitter Campaign', BBC Three (17 Oct. 2017), https://www.bbc.co.uk/bbcthree/article/99087acf-d8c2-408b-8209-f22b7f633744

p. 134 **'we need to teach boys the lessons of Mr Yancy's article from an early age…** Rachel L. Harris and Lisa Tarchak, 'Taking Responsibility or a Requiem? Men Talk about #MeToo', *The New York Times* (10 Dec. 2018), https://www.nytimes.com/2018/12/10/opinion/men-talk-about-metoo-women.html

p. 141 **In a piece that I read about the need for men to listen to female experiences of #MeToo, published in the *Independent* on 20 October 2018…** Harriet Hall, 'Now Is Not the Time For Men To Speak About How Hard MeToo Is for Them. Now Is the Time for Men to Listen', *Independent* (20 Oct. 2018), https://www.independent.co.uk/voices/metoo-men-reaction-sexual-assault-rape-womens-rights-richard-cooke-a8593366.html

p. 142 **Another *Independent* piece, which explored male violence as a product of toxic masculinity, resulted in hundreds of outraged comments…** Janey Stephenson, 'It's Not Muslims or People with Mental Health Problems Who Are Most Likely to Kill You in a Terrorist Attack – It's Men', *Independent* (27 Jul. 2016), https://www.independent.co.uk/voices/terrorist-attack-muslims-mentally-ill-japan-france-germany-men-its-toxic-masculinity-a7158156.html

p. 142 **As Dave Chappelle says, 'You got all the bad guys scared, and that's good'…** Katie Kilkenny, 'Dave Chappelle Jokes that Louis C.K. Accuser Has a "Brittle Ass Spirit" in Netflix Special', *Hollywood Reporter* (31 Dec. 2017), https://www.hollywoodreporter.com/news/dave-chappelle-jokes-louis-ck-accuser-has-a-brittle-ass-spirit-netflix-special-1070882

p. 143 **one in three women will suffer physical or sexual violence at some point in their lives…** UN News, 'A Staggering One-in-Three Women, Experience Physical, Sexual Abuse', *UN News*, 24 November 2019, https://news.un.org/en/story/2019/11/1052041

p. 143 **that two women in the UK die every day from domestic violence**… Refuge, 'The Extent of Domestic Violence', *Refuge*, https://www.refuge.org.uk/our-work/forms-of-violence-and-abuse/domestic-violence/domestic-violence-the-facts/

p. 143 **that the leading cause of death for a pregnant woman in the US is homicide…** Michael Alison Chandler, 'Maryland Case Underscores Fact That Homicide Is a Top Cause of Death for Pregnant Women', *The Washington Post* (15 Sep. 2017), https://www.washingtonpost.com/local/social-issues/maryland-case-undercores-fact-that-homicide-is-a-top-cause-of-death-for-pregnant-women/2017/09/15/9c4d5b62-9a39-11e7-87fc-c3f7ee4035c9_story.html

p. 143 **If we cannot heal what we cannot feel…** bell hooks, *The Will to Change: Men, Masculinity and Love*, Atria Books: New York (2004)

p. 144 **'It's hard to be a man these days. I feel like a lot of us feel like we're under attack…** Joanna Robinson and Julie Miller, 'William H. Macy Sees Both Sides of Time's Up: "It's Hard to Be a Man These Days"', *Vanity Fair* (22 Jan. 2018), https://www.vanityfair.com/hollywood/2018/01/william-h-macy-sag-awards-times-up-its-hard-to-be-a-man

p. 144 **In a recent collaboration between GQ and *Glamour* magazine, where over 1,000 men were surveyed…** GQ, 'What 1,147 Men Think About #MeToo: A Glamour x GQ Survey', GQ (30 May 2018), https://www.gq.com/story/metoo-and-men-survey-glamour-gq

p. 144 **Benjy Hansen-Bundy mused that 'I think guys are still a little wary. One guy wrote, "The movement doesn't come across as inclusive to men." To be honest, I feel some of that trepidation too…** Justine Harman and Benjy Hansen-Bundy, 'What 1,147 Men Really Think About #MeToo', *Glamour* (30 May 2018), https://www.glamour.com/story/men-metoo-survey-glamour-gq

p. 147 **'They argue that she drank beer, she danced with her attacker and, therefore, she wanted sex…** Laurie Halse Anderson, 'I've Talked With Teenage Boys About Sexual Assault for 20 Years. This Is What They Still Don't Know', *Time* (15 Jan. 2019), https://time.com/5503804/ive-talked-with-teenage-boys-about-sexual-assault-for-20-years-this-is-what-they-still-dont-know/

p. 147 **When a boy says these things, the girls in the class are shocked, and the teacher is appalled...** Ibid.

p. 147 **Ralph Jones, writing in the *Telegraph*, reports that young men feel angst-ridden and are 'looking for guidance or reassurance'...** Ralph Jones, 'Why Men Are So Unhappy Right Now – and Can Jordan Peterson Really Help Them?', *Telegraph* (8 May 2019), https://www.telegraph.co.uk/men/thinking-man/culture-warrior-jordan-peterson-became-cult-hit-young-men/

p. 147 **Alyssa Milano pointed out 'my kid in school learns that if his clothes catch on fire'...** *Good Morning America* (2017), ABC, https://www.youtube.com/watch?v=hyMG0hXMR6g

p. 149 **'The pessimist thinks of Weinstein, calling up Peter Jackson and suggesting that he might not want to hire Ashley Judd or Mira Sorvino for *The Lord of the Rings*'...** 'Weinstein "Derailed My Career" Sorvino Says after Peter Jackson Claim', *BBC News* (16 Dec. 2017), https://www.bbc.co.uk/news/entertainment-arts-42377607

p. 150 **In a 2018 survey for the Young Women's Trust, a quarter of the women interviewed said that they would be reluctant to report harassment for fear of losing their job...** Emily Burt, 'Quarter of Young Women Fear They Would Lose Their Job If They Reported Sexual Harassment', *People Management* (13 Sep. 2018), https://www.peoplemanagement.co.uk/news/articles/quarter-young-women-fear-lose-job-reported-sexual-harassment

p. 150 **in a 2018 survey by Women for Women International, not a single woman in Nigeria or Afghanistan had ever heard of the #MeToo movement...** Maya Oppenheim, '"#MeToo Has Not Gone Far Enough": Survey Finds Movement Virtually Unheard of by Women in Developing Countries', *Independent* (8 Mar. 2019), https://www.independent.co.uk/news/world/international-womens-day-metoo-afghanistan-nigeria-assault-a8812121.html

p. 150 **In France, 93 per cent of complaints against sexual harassment are dropped or never followed up by law enforcement...** Alissa J. Rubin, '"Revolt" in France Against

Sexual Harassment Hits Cultural Resistance', *New York Times* (19 Nov. 2017), https://www.nytimes.com/2017/11/19/world/europe/france-sexual-harassment.html

p. 151 **Harvey Weinstein was sentenced to twenty-three years in prison by Judge James Burke at the New York County Supreme Court...** Lauren Aratani and Ed Pilkington, 'Harvey Weinstein Sentenced to 23 Years in Prison on Rape Conviction', *Guardian* (11 Mar. 2020), https://www.theguardian.com/world/2020/mar/11/harvey-weinstein-sentencing-rape-conviction

p. 151 **California governor Jerry Brown signed two bills inspired by the case...** Jazmine Ulloa, 'Spurred by Brock Turner Case, Gov. Jerry Brown Signs Laws to Toughen Laws against Rape', *Los Angeles Times* (30 Sep. 2016), https://www.latimes.com/politics/la-pol-sac-california-sex-crimes-stanford-cosby-bills-20160930-snap-htmlstory.html

p. 151 **Aaron Persky, the judge who sentenced Turner, was recalled by voters in June 2018...** Maggie Astor, 'California Voters Remove Judge Aaron Persky, Who Gave a 6-Month Sentence for Sexual Assault', *New York Times* (6 Jun. 2018), https://www.nytimes.com/2018/06/06/us/politics/judge-persky-brock-turner-recall.html

p. 151 **In September 2018, California banned silence clauses in cases involving sexual harassment...** Stacy Perman, '#MeToo law Restricts Use of Nondisclosure Agreements in Sexual Misconduct Cases', *Los Angeles Times* (31 Dec. 2018), https://www.latimes.com/business/hollywood/la-fi-ct-nda-hollywood-20181231-story.html

p. 152 **In Tel Aviv, a new programme has been introduced to deal with domestic abuse...** Jana Kasperkevic, 'Private Violence: Up to 75% of Abused Women Who Are Murdered Are Killed after They Leave Their Partners', *Guardian* (20 Oct. 2014), https://www.theguardian.com/money/us-money-blog/2014/oct/20/domestic-private-violence-women-men-abuse-hbo-ray-rice

p. 152 **In Greece, the criminal code has been amended to recognize in law that sex without consent is rape...** Amnesty International, 'Greece: Newly Amended Rape Law Is a Historic Victory for Women', *Amnesty International* (6 Jun.

2019), https://www.amnesty.org/en/latest/news/2019/06/greece-newly-amended-rape-law-is-a-historic-victory-for-women/

p. 152 **The social activism group A Call to Men...** Rebecca Seales, 'What Has #MeToo Actually Changed?', *BBC News* (12 May 2018), https://www.bbc.co.uk/news/world-44045291

p. 152 **Nearly 60 per cent of voters thought that Kavanaugh lied under oath...** Anna North, 'New Poll Shows Major Shift in How Americans Think about Men in Power', *Vox* (27 Sep. 2019), https://www.vox.com/2019/9/27/20885011/trump-brett-kavanaugh-me-too-metoo-2020

p. 152 **And 50 per cent said that the hearings had made them think more about the fact that men have more power in government than women...** Ibid.

p. 152 **In a later survey by PerryUndem, 49 per cent of voters said that they wanted more women elected as a result of Kavanaugh's appointment...** Ibid.

p. 153 **'The last and most important thing I can say is just think about it...** Drew Schwartz, 'Dan Harmon Explains Exactly How He Harassed a Female "Community" Writer', *Vice* (12 Jan. 2018), https://www.vice.com/en_uk/article/a3nydj/dan-harmon-explains-exactly-how-he-harassed-female-community-writer-vgtrn

p. 153 **'What are women now?' a #MeToo sceptic has asked...** 'Jordan Peterson on the #MeToo Moment', *National Post* (24 Mar. 2018), https://www.youtube.com/watch?v=g8GSlP2yCD8